P9-DUU-736

SPECTRUM®

Test Prep

Grade 6

WITHDRAWN

GIFT OF THE FRIENDS
OF THE WALNUT CREEK LIBRARY

Published by Spectrum®
An imprint of Carson-Dellosa Publishing LLC
Greensboro, North Carolina

Spectrum®
An imprint of Carson-Dellosa Publishing LLC
P.O. Box 35665
Greensboro, NC 27425 USA

© 2015 Carson-Dellosa Publishing LLC. Except as permitted under the United States Copyright Act, no part of this publication may be reproduced, stored, or distributed in any form or by any means (mechanically, electronically, recording, etc.) without the prior written consent of Carson-Dellosa Publishing LLC. Spectrum® is an imprint of Carson-Dellosa Publishing LLC.

Printed in the USA • All rights reserved.

ISBN 978-1-4838-1379-0

02-068157811

Table of Contents

What's Inside?

Spectrum Test Prep is designed to help you and your sixth grader prepare and plan for success on standardized tests.

Strategies

This workbook is structured around strategies. A strategy is a careful plan or method for achieving a particular goal, such as succeeding on a test. Strategies can be broad general strategies about test as a whole or a category of skills. Strategies can also be specific, providing step-by-step instructions on how to tackle a problem or offering guidelines on how to answer a question about a story. Learning how to apply a strategy gives test-takers a plan for how to approach a test as a whole and how to answer questions.

This workbook offers a set of broader strategies as well as very specific strategies. General test-taking strategies apply to all tests, and should be used to help prepare for the test. Specific strategies for English Language Arts and Mathematics tests are divided into larger categories of skills students will encounter, such as reading literature or performing calculations. On each practice page, you will find even more specific strategies that apply to the skills.

Test Tips

Test Tips are included throughout the practice pages. While strategies offer a plan for answering test items, Test Tips offer ideas for how to apply each strategy or how to approach a type of question. There are general Test Tips that apply to all tests as well as specific Test Tips for English Language Arts and Mathematics tests.

Practice Pages

The workbook is divided into two sections, English Language Arts and Mathematics. Each section has practice activities that have questions similar to those that will appear on standardized tests. Also included are strategies and Test Tips to guide students. Students should use a pencil to complete these activities.

Strategy Review Pages

Strategy review pages give your student an opportunity to review and practice important strategies in each content area. These strategies cover the important skills students will encounter on tests in English Language Arts and Mathematics.

Answer Key

Answers for all of the practice pages and strategy review pages are found in an answer key at the end of the book.

Test-Taking Strategies

Being prepared is key to doing your best on test day. Read the tips below to help you prepare for tests.

In the days before the test...

- Keep up on your reading, worksheets, and assignments. Completing all your assigned work will help you be better prepared for the test.

- Don't wait until right before the test to review materials. Create a study schedule for the best result. That way, you can study a bit at a time and not all at once.

- Take advantage of sample items and practice tests. Complete these to practice for your test. If you run into concepts or skills that are new, ask a teacher or other adult.

The night before the test...

- Don't try to study everything all over again the night before. If you've been studying in the days before the test, all you need the night before is a light review of your notes. Remind yourself of the key ideas and practice a few skills, but don't study late into the night.

- Make sure you have all the materials you will need for the test, such as pencils, paper, and a calculator. Check with your teacher to make sure you know what tools to bring. Having everything ready the night before will make the morning less stressful.

- Get a good night's sleep the night before the test. If you are well rested, you will be more alert and able to do your best.

On the day of the test...

- Don't skip breakfast. If you are hungry, you won't be thinking about the test. You'll be thinking about lunch.

- Make sure you have at least two sharpened pencils with you and any other tools needed.

- Read all directions carefully. Make sure you understand how you are supposed to answer each question.

- For multiple choice questions, read all the possible answers before choosing one. If you know that some answers are wrong, cross them off. Even if you have to guess, this will eliminate some wrong answers.

- Once you choose or write an answer, double check it by reading the question again. Confirm that your answer is correct.

- Answer every part of a question. If a question asks you to show your work or to explain how you arrived at an answer, make sure you include that information.

- If you are stuck on a question, or unsure, mark it lightly with a pencil and move on. If you have time, you can come back. This is especially true on a timed test.

- Breathe! Remind yourself that you've prepared for the test and that you will do your best!

Strategies for English Language Arts Tests

Read the strategies below to learn more about how they work.

Use details from the text to make inferences, understand theme, and draw out meaning.
Writers carefully choose details to include in their writing. Every detail matters. Each one is included for a purpose. As you read stories, look for details that help you understand what the writer is saying about characters, events, and the overall meaning, or theme. As you read passages, look for details that give reasons that support any opinions or facts the writer shares, as well as the central or main idea.

Identify literary or structural elements and use them to understand the meaning of a text.
Writers use literary elements such as figurative language to bring more meaning to their writing. They choose a structure that reflects their purpose for writing. Read carefully for ways that these elements help you understand the meaning of a story, poem, or passage.

Look carefully at visuals such as illustrations, diagrams, or graphs to see how they connect to the text.
Visuals are always related to the text. It is up to readers to figure out the connection. Does the visual explain something that is difficult to say in words? Does it add detail? As you read stories and passages, look carefully at visuals to see what information they provide.

Reread texts to make comparisons, draw conclusions, or support inferences.
Every reader has his or her own ideas about a text. If you are asked to draw a conclusion about what the writer means or thinks, however, you need to rely on details in the text, not your own opinions. When you have drawn a conclusion or made an inference, reread the text to make sure you can support it with facts, examples, and other information from the text.

Use word clues in a text to identify its structure, to see how ideas in a text are related, and to clarify word meanings.
Some words are signals that a text has a particular structure. For example, the words *cause* and *because* often signal a cause-and-effect structure. You may also be able to use words as clues to the meaning of unfamiliar words.

When writing, use details to support, explain, or clarify your main ideas.
In persuasive and informational writing, it is important to make sure you support and explain each main idea with details. Facts, examples, and logical reasoning can all be used to make your main ideas strong and clear.

Use an outline to plan your writing.
Prewriting activities such as outlining can make writing clear and make your ideas easy to understand. A simple outline that lists main ideas or claims followed by their supporting details is enough to make your writing flow more easily.

Use transitions to show how ideas are related.
As you write, use transitions to help your reader follow your train of thought. You may know how your ideas are related, but readers need a little extra help! For example, the transition *As a result* shows that you are explaining a cause and an effect. The transitions *Next* and *Finally* help readers see that you are explaining a process or events that happen in a certain order.

Revise to make sure your writing is clear and makes sense. Then, edit to fix errors.
After you finish your draft, you may have time to revise and edit. First, revise to make sure your words say what you wanted them to say. Then, check spelling, capitalization, punctuation, and grammar to catch and fix errors.

Name _____ Date _____

English Language Arts

Cite Text Evidence to Support Inferences
Reading: Literature

DIRECTIONS: Read the story.

Time to Win

[1] In one of the closest games of the season, the teams were so evenly matched that neither team had been able to score, and now, time was running out. [2] No score would mean exciting (and exhausting) overtime play, but fans and players knew that one precise kick would settle the competition. [3] Justin's feet pounded the soccer field toward the goal, and his heart pounded along with the rhythm of his steps.

[4] "I'm open!" he shouted. [5] "Pass the ball!" [6] He scanned the field, searching for a player from his team.

[7] "Brian, over here!" [8] Marco kicked the ball toward Justin, but before Justin could reach it, one of the opponents darted in and booted the ball away. [9] "Don't worry—we'll get it next time!" hollered the coach, as Marco sprinted back to regain possession of the ball. [10] This time, Marco dribbled out the wing, beating opponent after opponent. [11] He centered the ball, and Justin bolted just in time to kick it toward the goal. [12] The vigilant goalie, alert to possible game-ending shots, scooped up the ball and threw it back into play.

[13] "Nice try! [14] You almost had it!" shouted the coach as the team rushed back down the field to counter their opponents, who now had possession. [15] An opposing player slipped past the first defender and took a shot at the goal but missed.

[16] "Make this one count!" bellowed the goalie as he kicked the ball to his team. [17] Marco marshaled his energy and focus, determined to shake up the scoreless game while the clock relentlessly ticked down. [18] As he darted down the field, he could hear the fans in the background roaring, "Go! Score!"

[19] Hurling their remaining strength into a last effort, the whole team charged down to help him. [20] They passed the ball around the opponents, maneuvering closer and closer to the goal. [21] Justin passed the ball to Marco, who took aim at the goal and blasted the ball with all the force he could muster just as the final seconds flickered across the field clock. [22] The shot was good—the team had won!

[23] "Congratulations! [24] You guys were great! [25] What a game! [26] What a team!" cheered the fans. [27] Justin and Marco exchanged a traditional high five and beamed with pride as the exultant team headed over to congratulate their opponents on a fiercely fought match.

Strategy
Use details about the characters' actions, words, and thoughts to make inferences about the characters.

1. **At the beginning of the story, Justin hopes to score the winning goal. At the end of the story, Marco scores the winning goal. What evidence supports the inference that Justin is not disappointed? Choose two correct answers.**

   (A) Justin's shot is intercepted by the goalie.

   (B) Justin's coach yells encouraging words to him.

   (C) Justin's teammates congratulate their opponents.

   (D) Justin and Marco exchange a high five after the game.

   (E) Justin passes the ball to Marco as the clock ticks down.

English Language Arts

Cite Text Evidence to Support Inferences
Reading: Literature

DIRECTIONS: Use the story to choose or write the correct answer.

Strategy To make an inference, ask yourself what you don't know about characters or events.

Test Tip Make an inference by using what you already know from experience and common sense, and what happens in the story.

2. **What detail in the story helps to clarify the meaning of vigilant in Sentence 12?**

   (A) Justin's heart pounds as he rushes the goalie.

   (B) Marco's game-winning goal gets past the goalie.

   (C) The goalie is "alert to possible game-ending shots."

   (D) The goalie bellows at his team to "Make this one count!"

3. **Write a sentence that makes an inference about Justin and Marco's coach. Include quoted words from the story to support your inference.**

   Test Tip
   Be sure to quote the words exactly and place them inside quotation marks.

   _____

   _____

   _____

   _____

   _____

   _____

4. **Which detail most strongly suggests that all the players on the field are talented?**

   (A) The fans cheer, "What a game!" after the winning goal.

   (B) Both teams have prevented goals for most of the game.

   (C) The winning team congratulates the losing team after the game.

   (D) The narrator describes overtime play as "exciting (but exhausting)."

5. **Choose two sentences that readers could cite to support the inference that the players are exhausted as the game time runs out.**

   (A) Sentence 1

   (B) Sentence 9

   (C) Sentence 17

   (D) Sentence 19

   (E) Sentence 20

   Write how you know.

   _____

   _____

   _____

   _____

6. **Explain why it is important to use quotes from the story when making an inference.**

   _____

   _____

   _____

   _____

English Language Arts

Determine Theme and Summarize
Reading: Literature

DIRECTIONS: Read the story. Then, answer the questions.

[1] Daedalus felt the walls closing in around him, but he pushed his fears down. [2] He could not let his son, Icarus, see his panic; he had to comfort the boy and keep him safe. [3] Yet, trapped in his own trap, Daedalus knew their situation was dire.

[4] Years ago, the great inventor and architect had created the Labyrinth for King Minos. [5] It was hard to turn a person of Minos's power down, but if Daedalus had known Minos's intentions, he would have fled before agreeing to do the work. [6] The Labyrinth's twisting paths could not be retraced; someone thrown into the prison died there able to see the sky above but never reach it. [7] And now that someone was Daedalus, the latest victim of the king's rage.

[8] But, being Daedalus, he was never far from a plan of action. [9] "Icarus," he said gently, so as not to frighten the child, "gather as many feathers as you can find." [10] The boy played at finding feathers fallen from birds as they soared over the serpentine prison, and the father molded them into wings held in place by warmed candle wax. [11] Soon, two pairs of wings were ready. [12] Daedalus attached wings to himself and his son, warning, "Icarus, fly low, near the water, as we escape. [13] The sun will melt the wax if you fly too high." [14] Alas, as he flew, the joy of escape and the delight of soaring like a bird inspired Icarus to fly up, up, up—until the heat made his wings melt away, and he plunged into the sea forever, as his grieving father flew on to safety.

Strategy
Identify plot elements to help summarize a story, and identify its theme or themes.

1. **Explain in your own words the problem Daedalus faces.**

He built a ____yth ___
___king ___ ___ ___
____ped ___ ___ h ___
son.

2. **Which two sentences tell readers why Daedalus does not give up as he faces the problem?**

   (A) Sentence 2
   (B) Sentence 3
   (C) Sentence 6
   (D) Sentence 8

English Language Arts

Determine Theme and Summarize
Reading: Literature

DIRECTIONS: Use the story to choose or write the best answer.

Strategy

Ask, *What do the characters' struggles suggest about life or about being human?* The answer to this question helps you determine the theme.

3. **Which statement captures a theme of the story of Daedalus and Icarus?**

   (A) Powerful kings are easy to anger.

   (B) Inventions solve many life problems.

   (C) Freedom is more important than a king's favor.

   (D) Children should heed their parents' wise advice.

Test Tip

Outline a story's three main sections by asking, *What problem do the characters face? What challenges must the characters face as they try to solve the problem? How do the characters solve the problem?* These questions help you summarize the story.

Write how you know.

_____

_____

_____

_____

_____

_____

_____

_____

4. **Summarize the story of Daedalus and Icarus. Include the major plot events only.**

_____

_____

_____

_____

_____

_____

_____

_____

_____

_____

_____

_____

Name _____ Date _____

Interpret Figurative Language
Reading: Literature

DIRECTIONS: Read the poem. Then, answer the questions.

**from *The Jungle Book*
by *Rudyard Kipling***
NOW this is the law of the jungle, as old and as true as the sky,
And the wolf that shall keep it may prosper, but the wolf that shall break it must die.

As the creeper[1] that girdles the tree trunk, the law runneth forward and back;
For the strength of the pack is the wolf, and the strength of the wolf is the pack.

Wash daily from nose tip to tail tip; drink deeply, but never too deep;
And remember the night is for hunting and forget not the day is for sleep.

The jackal may follow the tiger, but, cub, when thy whiskers are grown,
Remember the wolf is a hunter—go forth and get food of thy own.
  [1] *creeper—vine*

Strategy — Identify examples of figurative language and interpret them to better understand the meaning of a story or poem.

Test Tip — Remember that metaphors, similes, and personification all compare seemingly different things to show how they are alike. Identify what is being compared, and determine how the writer uses the comparison.

1. **Part A: Which word in Line 2 shows that the meaning of prosper contrasts with the meaning of die?**

   (A) wolf

   (B) keep

   (C) but

   (D) must

   Write how you know.

   _____

   _____

   _____

   _____

   Part B: Choose three actions that are the actions of a wolf that prospers.

   (A) lives a short life

   (B) follows the tiger

   (C) keeps itself clean

   (D) hunts successfully

   (E) creeps around a tree

   (F) obeys the law of the jungle

2. **What do the last two suggest about the narrator of the poem? Explain who is narrating and why.**

   _____

   _____

   _____

   _____

Name _____ Date _____

English Language Arts

Interpret Figurative and Connotative Language
Reading: Literature

DIRECTIONS: Read the poem. Then, answer the questions that follow.

from "The Brook"
by Alfred, Lord Tennyson

I steal by lawns and grassy plots,
I slide by hazel covers[1];
I move the sweet forget-me-nots[2]
That grow for happy lovers.

I slip, I slide, I gloom, I glance,
Among my skimming swallows;
I make the netted sunbeam dance
Against my sandy shallows.

I murmur under moon and stars
In brambly wildernesses;
I linger by my shingly bars[3];
I loiter round my cresses[4];

And out again I curve and flow
To join the brimming river,
For men may come and men may go,
But I go on for ever.

[1] *covers* — thick, intertwined vines
[2] *forget-me-nots* — small flowers
[3] *shingly bars* — covered in pebbles
[4] *cresses* — leafy plants

Strategy   Use literal or dictionary definitions to understand the meaning of words and phrases. Then, ask yourself what else the word or phrase means to find the deeper, connotative meaning.

Test Tip   Connotative meanings go beyond the dictionary definitions. For example, *He placed the book on the counter* has a neutral connotation, while *He slammed the book on the counter* has a negative connotation.

1. **What does the word *steal* mean in the context of first line?**

   (A) a useful and strong metal

   (B) to move cleverly and quietly

   (C) to take what belongs to another

   (D) a good price for something valuable

   Write how you know.

   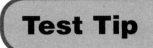

   _____

   _____

   _____

2. **Personification allows _____ to speak in the poem.**

   (A) the poet

   (B) the brook

   (C) a happy child

   (D) a skimming swallow

3. **How would this poem be different if the brook wasn't the narrator or character? What if the author chose not to use personification and just describe the brook himself?**

   _____

   _____

   _____

English Language Arts

Describe Connections Among Plot Events
Reading: Literature

DIRECTIONS: Read the story.

The Escape

[1] Into the shady glen, the small figure rode on a pony little larger than a dog. [2] The green-mantled figure patted the neck of the beast, whispering words of comfort into the animal's ear.

[3] "We've left the raiders behind, old friend," said Rowan, as she removed her hooded mantle. [4] Rowan was one of four daughters of Sylvia, guide of all wood folk.

[5] Suddenly, shouts of rough men cut through the glade's peace.

[6] "In here, I tell ya. [7] The maid's gone to hiding in this grove."

[8] "Nah, ya lunk. [9] She'd never wait for us here. [10] Not after she dunked old Stefan at the marsh. [11] No! [12] She's a gone on to her crazy folk, don'tcha know."

[13] The two gray-cloaked riders dismounted, still arguing as they examined the earth for traces of the child's flight. [14] "Who was the lout who let her escape?" asked the first.

[15] "'Tis one who no longer breathes the air so freely," returned the second grimly. [16] "The lord nearly choked the fool, even as the knave begged for mercy. [17] Ah, there's little patience for one who lets a mystic escape, to be true!"

[18] Five nobly dressed horsemen wove through the trees to the clearing where these two rustics still squatted. [19] In the lead came the fierce lord, a huge form with scarlet and gray finery worn over his coat of mail.

[20] "What say you?" he roared. [21] "Have you found the trail of Rowan?"

[22] "No, sire," spoke the first gray, trembling, "though I was certain the child headed into this wood. [23] Shall I continue to search, Lord?"

[24] "Aye, indeed," replied the master calmly, controlled. [25] "She is here. [26] I know it too. [27] You have a keen sense for the hunt, Mikkel. [28] Be at ready with your blade. [29] And you too, Short Brush! [30] Though a child, our Rowan is vicious with her weapon."

[31] "Yes, sire," agreed Mikkel and Short Brush.

[32] The two grays beat the bushes in the search. [33] Closer and closer they came to the child's hiding place, a small earthen scoop created when the roots of a wind-blown tree pulled free of the earth. [34] The evil lord and his lot remained mounted, ready to pursue should the young girl take flight once more. [35] And so, they were not prepared for the child's play.

[36] Rowan softly, softly sang, "You wind-whipped branches, shudder, shake. [37] You oaks and cedars, tremble. [38] Take these men and beasts who do us wrong. [39] Not in these woods do they belong."

[40] As a mighty gust of wind roared, nearby trees slapped their branches to the point of breaking, reaching out and grasping the mounted men. [41] As their lord, seeing the danger, spurred his horse to flee, an immense gaping cavern opened in the trunk of an ancient oak and swallowed his surprised mail-clad men whole.

[42] Mikkel and Short Brush, meanwhile, were lifted high into the air by a white pine and a blue spruce. [43] Lifted high . . . held high . . . for a while.

[44] "Return from whence you came. [45] Go to your families, and tell them of the wrath of Sylvia," commanded Rowan. [46] "She would not wish you to come to her land again!"

[47] The pine and spruce tossed the two gray trackers over the trees of the forest and into the field beyond. [48] The field was already harvested and soggy with the rains of autumn. [49] Mikkel and Short Brush, unhurt but shaken by their arboreal flight, rose and fled immediately to tell their master of the strange doings of this wood.

English Language Arts

Describe Connections Among Characters and Plot Events
Reading: Literature

DIRECTIONS: Use the story to answer the questions.

Strategy	As you read a story, ask questions that help you make connections between events. Ask yourself, *Why do events happen? What causes one event, and what happens next?* Think about how one event leads to others.

Test Tip	When you need to answer questions about plot, read the story twice—first, to read it as a whole story, and second, to outline the plot. Group events under three main sections of plot: introduction of characters and conflict, development of conflict, and resolution of conflict.

1. Who are the characters in the story?

_____

_____

_____

2. Describe the setting of the story.

_____

_____

_____

_____

3. Part A: Why is the lord who wears scarlet and gray hunting for Rowan?

(A) Rowan is related to the lord.

(B) Rowan has mystical powers.

(C) Rowan stabbed one of his men.

(D) Rowan has been taken prisoner by Sylvia.

Write how you know.

_____

_____

_____

_____

Part B: Which sentence from the story contains details that explain why the lord is hunting for Rowan?

(A) Sentence 10

(B) Sentence 17

(C) Sentence 30

(D) Sentence 33

4. Part A: Why do the trackers and mounted pursuers obey the lord without question? Choose two.

(A) They admire and trust him.

(B) They share his anger at Rowan.

(C) They fear he will be angry with them.

(D) They know he will reward those who aid him.

English Language Arts

Describe Connections Among Characters and Plot Events

Reading: Literature

DIRECTIONS: Use the story to answer the questions.

Strategy — As you read, ask yourself, *Who are the people in this story? What are they like?*

Test Tip — A character's traits shape how they respond to events in a story. A forgiving character may overlook a mistake, for example, or a proud character may react badly to an insult.

Part B: Write a detail from the story that supports your answer to Part A.

_____

_____

_____

_____

_____

_____

_____

_____

_____

_____

5. As Rowan deals with the story's conflict, what actions does she take that reveal her unusual powers? Use at least two details from the story to support your answer.

_____

_____

_____

_____

_____

6. How can kidnapping Rowan help the fierce lord? Use details about the characters in the story.

_____

_____

_____

_____

7. Which sentence describes the relationship Rowan has with nature?

Ⓐ She can control weather and plants.

Ⓑ She avoids natural elements.

Ⓒ She is afraid of the trees and wind.

Ⓓ She wants nature to be afraid of her.

Write how you know.

_____

_____

_____

_____

8. Knowing what you know about the character Rowan, are other characters afraid of her?

_____

_____

_____

English Language Arts

Describe Connections Among Characters and Plot Events

Reading: Literature

DIRECTIONS: Use the story to answer the questions.

Strategy — While reading, identify events that build on each other, such as events that are suspenseful or exciting, or events that are caused by characters or setting.

9. **What inference can readers make about why Rowan "dunked old Stefan at the marsh"?**

(A) Stefan attacked her pony.

(B) Stefan wanted to use her magic.

(C) She was playing games with Stefan.

(D) She was trying to escape from Stefan.

What details helped you make this inference?

_____

_____

_____

_____

_____

_____

Test Tip

A story's plot includes the events that happen to characters. Sometimes, events happen on their own, because of who the character is. Sometimes, characters actions cause events to happen.

10. **Explain the plot of the story. Use details from the story.**

_____

_____

_____

_____

_____

_____

_____

11. **What will Mikkel and Short Brush, who land in the field "unhurt but shaken," likely advise the lord to do when they report to him?**

(A) Help his men escape from the oak tree.

(B) Return to the forest to hunt Rowan.

(C) Respect the power of Sylvia and leave Rowan alone.

(D) Take more knights with him the next time he enters the forest.

What details support your answer?

_____

_____

_____

_____

_____

_____

_____

_____

Analyze Text Structure
Reading: Literature

DIRECTIONS: Read the opening scene of a play.

> ### from "Trifles" by Susan Glaspell
>
> [SCENE: *The kitchen in the now-abandoned farmhouse of John Wright, a gloomy kitchen, and left in disorder—unwashed pans under the sink, a loaf of bread outside the breadbox, a dishtowel on the table—other signs of incomplete work. At the rear, the outer door opens, and the SHERIFF comes in followed by the COUNTY ATTORNEY and HALE. The sheriff and Hale are men in middle life, and the county attorney is a young man; all are bundled and go to the stove at once. They are followed by two women—the SHERIFF'S WIFE first; she is a slight, wiry woman with a thin, nervous face. MRS. HALE is larger and would ordinarily be called more comfortable looking, but she is disturbed now and looks fearfully about as she enters. The women have come in slowly and stand close together near the door.*]
>
> [1] COUNTY ATTORNEY [*rubbing his hands*]. This feels good. Come up to the fire, ladies.
>
> [2] [*after taking a step forward*]. I'm not—cold.
>
> [3] SHERIFF [*unbuttoning his overcoat and stepping away from the stove, as if to mark the beginning of official business*]. Now, Mr. Hale, before we move things about, you explain to Mr. Henderson just what you saw when you came here yesterday morning.
>
> [4] COUNTY ATTORNEY. By the way, has anything been moved? Are things just as you left them yesterday?
>
> [5] SHERIFF [*looking about*]. It's just the same. When it dropped below zero last night, I thought I'd better send Frank this morning to make a fire for us—no use getting pneumonia while on a big case, but I told him not to touch anything except the stove—and you know Frank.
>
> [6] COUNTY ATTORNEY. Somebody should have stayed here yesterday.
>
> [7] SHERIFF. Oh—yesterday. . . . I knew you could get back from Omaha by today, and as long as I went over everything here myself—
>
> [8] COUNTY ATTORNEY. Well, Mr. Hale, tell us what happened when you came here yesterday morning.

Strategy | Use features or elements of a play to draw out more meaning from a play, such as dialogue markers and stage directions.

Test Tip | Dialogue markers tell who is speaking. Stage directions—descriptions of what characters do and how they move and speak—are often in italics or inside parentheses.

1. **Read the stage directions, paying attention to how the characters are dressed and what they do when they enter the house. What do the stage directions tell you about the play's setting?**

   (A) It is set in the winter and in the past.

   (B) It is set in a big city and in the present.

   (C) It is set long ago in a make-believe land.

   (D) It is set in a farmhouse and in the future.

   Write how you know.

   _____
   _____
   _____
   _____
   _____
   _____

Analyze Text Structure
Reading: Literature

DIRECTIONS: Use the play to choose or write the best answer.

> **Strategy** — Use the parts of a story, play, or poem to help you identify the theme, setting, or plot. Look for the setting and plot events in the stage directions of a play. Look at the dialogue to find details about plot and theme.

> **Test Tip** — Compare the format of a play to a story to help you understand its parts. For example, a story has paragraphs, a play has scenes, and a poem has stanzas.

2. The stage directions describe the characters—who they are and, in some cases, how they feel. These clues suggest that people have come to the house to

   (A) investigate a crime

   (B) get warm by the stove

   (C) clean up the messy kitchen

   (D) find out where the homeowners are

   Write how you know.

   _____

   _____

   _____

   _____

   _____

   _____

3. Read lines 7 and 8 again. What does the long dash at the end of line 7 tell readers?

   (A) The attorney interrupts the sheriff.

   (B) The sheriff has finished speaking.

   (C) The sheriff notices that something was moved in the room.

   (D) The attorney thinks the women have moved things in the room.

4. Reread lines 1 and 2, and look at the stage directions. What do the stage directions *"after taking a step forward"* and the sheriff's wife Mrs. Peters' reply suggest about her?

   (A) For some reason, she is not cold like the others are.

   (B) For some reason, she is not aware that the sheriff is being polite.

   (C) For some reason, she does not want to walk farther into the kitchen.

   (D) For some reason, she does not like the sheriff or the county attorney.

5. Look at the dialogue markers in these lines. What do they suggest about which characters are in charge in the scene? Explain how you know.

   _____

   _____

   _____

   _____

   _____

   _____

   _____

   _____

   _____

English Language Arts

Explain the Narrator's Point of View
Reading: Literature

DIRECTIONS: Read the story. Then, answer the questions.

> [1] A fox caught in a trap escaped but, in so doing, lost his tail. [2] Thereafter, feeling his life a burden from the shame and ridicule to which he was exposed, he schemed to convince the other foxes that being tailless was much more attractive, thus making up for his deprivation. [3] He assembled a good many foxes and publicly advised them to cut off their tails, saying they would not only look much better without them, but they would also get rid of the weight of the brush, which was a great inconvenience. [4] One of them, interrupting him, said, "If you had not, yourself, lost your tail, my friend, you would not thus counsel us."

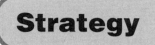 **Strategy** — Identify a narrator's point of view by reading story details carefully and looking for clues to who is telling the story. Then, think about how point of view affects the way the story is told.

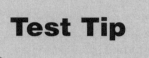 **Test Tip** — A first-person narrator knows only his or her own thoughts. Just as real people do, this narrator must infer other people's thoughts from what they do and say. When you read first-person point of view stories, ask, *Is the narrator guessing other characters' thoughts correctly?*

1. **Part A: What point of view does the narrator use to tell the story of the fox and his tail?**

   (A) first person, as the fox himself

   (B) third person, as the other foxes

   (C) third person, as someone outside the events

   (D) first person, as the hunter who set the trap

   Part B: Explain how you know.

   _____

   _____

   _____

   _____

   _____

   _____

   _____

2. **Which statement describes the narrator's attitude toward the fox?**

   (A) The narrator feels sorry for the fox because he lost his tail.

   (B) The narrator agrees with the fox that it is better to do without a tail.

   (C) The narrator thinks it was silly of the fox to let his tail get caught in the trap.

   (D) The narrator disapproves of the fox's trick to get other foxes to cut off their tails.

3. **Explain how the story would be different if it were told in the opposite point of view.**

   _____

   _____

   _____

   _____

   _____

Name _____ Date 1-2-20

English Language Arts

Explain the Narrator's Point of View
Reading: Literature

DIRECTIONS: Read the story. Then, answer the questions that follow.

> [5] "Ouch! [6] Ouch!" I cried, turning to see what was the matter. [7] "Oh, my tail—my fine, brushy, glossy tail is caught in a hunter's trap. [8] Wait up, fellows!" [9] My friends ran on ahead, for the hunters were close behind. [10] I gave a mighty yank to free myself and did—but not all of myself. [11] My beautiful tail was caught, and I fled without it.
>
> [12] When I caught up to my friends hidden in our dark den, what a laugh they had at my expense. [13] "Who's got your tail?" they laughed, rolling about with the humor of it. [14] "Some fine lady, I guess, who'll wear it around her neck!"
>
> [15] "Who needs a tail anyway?" I replied, trying to sound pleased. [16] "I'm glad to be rid of it—always in the way, always getting caught in vines and brambles. [17] If I were you, I'd lose the tail today."

Strategy
When reading a story told in first-person point of view, look closely for details that state what the narrator truly thinks and feels. The narrator may say things that do not match how he or she feels.

Test Tip
First-person narrators refer to themselves as *I* and *me*: "I turned in my work on time," I said. However, a third-person point of view refers to characters as *he* or *she* or *they*: "I turned in my work on time," he said. Look at the dialogue tags (*he said, she replied, they yelled, I answered*) for clues to the narrator's point of view.

1. **What point of view does this story's narrator use?**

   (A) first person, as the fox
   (B) third person, as the fox
   (C) first person, as someone outside the events
   (D) third person, as someone outside the events

   Write how you know.

   The fox describes how his tail was caught and he lost his tail.

   Because the fox or the narrator is using I , my tail & my friends

2. **Reread sentence 4 from the story on p. 19. Then, rewrite it from the point of view of the narrator of the second story.**

   My friend interferred and said, if you didn't lose your tail, you would not be talking to us.

4. **Which two sentences best explain why the fox pretends he doesn't mind losing his tail?**

   (A) He wants to hide his embarrassment.
   (B) He knows his tail isn't important.
   (C) He likes being teased by the foxes.
   (D) He needs the other foxes to like him.

Name _____ Date _____

English Language Arts

Compare Stories with Different Genres
Reading: Literature

DIRECTIONS: Read the poem. Then, answer the question that follows.

Cinderella, Waiting

"Have a loooovely evening," Sister sneered as they left,
Dangling laces and jewels, but of fashion bereft.
I sit in the ashes, broom and mop at my side,
Dirty with housework but still clutching my pride.
Fairy godmothers, I'm told, time their entrances well:
They swoop in, all golden, and cast the right spell
At just the precise instant, the girl gives up hope.

So, I wait in the dusk, wondering how I will cope
If the magic I long for leaves me in the lurch.
In the ashes I wait, by the cold hearth I perch,
Like a bird whose bright feathers have not yet appeared.
Do I see a faint glowing? Will the magic come near?

Strategy

Use your understanding of different genres to understand the meaning of what you read. Before you read, identify the genre: poem, story, myth, drama, or legend. Then, read with the traits of that genre in mind.

Test Tip

Genre, or type, of literature gives you clues about how to read. In a poem, you might find a story or an expression of a thought or feeling. A story will present a conflict and resolution, so look for these. The layout of a drama will make it clear who says what, but you'll have to make inferences about what the characters feel and why they do what they do.

1. **What features make the story above a poem?**

(A) lines, stanzas, rhymes

(B) magic, fairies, spells

(C) sentences, paragraphs

(D) characters, realistic events

Write how the poem would be structured differently if it were written as a story.

It would be like a
movie sricpt because
it has lots of dialouge
and actions.

Compare Stories with Different Genres
Reading: Literature

DIRECTIONS: Read the story. Then, answer the questions that follow.

> **Cinders, Done Waiting**
>
> [1] I've checked my smartphone, oh, a million times—no "Sorry I'm running a tad late" texts, so where is she already? [2] You know the deal, I know the deal, we all know the deal: The stepsisters head off to the ball, decked out in their "finery," so certain they'll be the ones to capture the prince's heart and hand. [3] (And which matters more to them, I wonder, his love or his kingdom?) [4] Meanwhile, I wait patiently in the kitchen until my fairy godmother sparkles into the room, waving her sparkly wand and shedding sparkly dust all over me until I'm gloriously clothed in a sparkling gown (and don't forget those sparkling glass shoes).
>
> [5] But Fairy Godmother is not anywhere to be found; the clock is ticking, the ball will be history before long.
>
> [6] Hmm . . . my smartphone—time to take matters into my own hands! First, an appropriate gown—let's see what's on sale. [7] Something in size perfect; how about in shocking neon purple? [8] There, that's the one—I'll show the lords and ladies how a girl gets attention at a ball. [9] Shoes next—forget glass! [10] Who in her right mind would wear breakable slippers? [11] I intend to dance until dawn, and I don't want to have to wear bandages afterward. [12] Got 'em! [13] And, finally, to book a limo . . . this is one princess-to-be who plans to arrive at the ball in style.
>
> [14] Look out, Prince—the Phoenix is about to rise from the ashes!

Strategy
Compare stories on the same theme. Use what you know about different genres to identify the theme. Then, compare how each story provides details about the theme.

Test Tip
Authors of poems and stories don't give the theme directly. Readers have to look for details and use what they already know to infer the theme.

2. **What is the main difference between the narrators—Cinderella and Cinders—in the two passages?**

   (A) Cinders admires her stepsisters' fashion senses, whereas Cinderella despises them.

   (B) Cinderella has faith that magic will save the day, whereas Cinders acts to make her own success.

   (C) Cinderella takes a comical view of her life, whereas Cinders is serious and sad about her situation.

   (●) Cinders wants to meet and dance with the Prince, whereas Cinderella merely wants to see the ball.

Quote lines or sentences from each passage that helped you choose the correct answer.

I intend to dance until dawn, and ladies how a girl gets attention in a ball to a prince.

[11]

English Language Arts

Compare Stories with Different Genres
Reading: Literature

DIRECTIONS: Use the poem and the story to answer the questions.

Strategy — To compare two stories, ask yourself how characters and events are the same and how they are different.

Test Tip — Try organizing your ideas in a chart or list. Then, review the information to make sure your ideas make sense.

3. **Complete the chart to compare the problem and resolution in the two passages.**

	CINDERELLA, WAITING	CINDERS, DONE WAITING
What problem does the narrator face?		
What is keeping the narrator from getting what she wants?		
What does the narrator choose to do about the problem?		
How is the problem resolved?		

4. **Which theme can apply to both the poem and the story?**

   (A) Waiting for something to happen is often difficult.

   (B) Patience will help you get what you want.

   (C) Wishing for events to occur is foolish.

   (D) Take action when you can.

Write how you know.

_____

_____

_____

English Language Arts

Compare Stories with Different Genres
Reading: Literature

DIRECTIONS: Use the poem and the story to answer the questions.

Strategy — Reread the beginning of each story you are comparing and see which details are the same. Continue for the middle and for the ending.

Test Tip — Poems convey a mood and tone, but stories and plays do, too. Different genres have unique features, but they have similarities, too. All tell a story.

5. **Which sentence describes the contrasting tones of the poem and story?**

   Ⓐ The poem is forceful, whereas the story is calm.

   Ⓑ The poem is angry, whereas the story is peaceful.

   Ⓒ The poem is full of hope, whereas the story is full of despair.

   Ⓓ The poem is full of longing, whereas the story is full of confidence.

   Write two details from the poem and two details from the story that convey tone.

   Poem:

   _____

   _____

   _____

   _____

   Story:

   _____

   _____

6. **Read sentences 2, 4, and 8 from the story. Then, read lines 1 and 3 of the poem. Based on these sentences, which inference can readers make about how the narrator in each passage feels about her stepsisters? Choose two.**

Ⓐ Both narrators usually ignore their stepsisters.

Ⓑ Both narrators love and are happy for their stepsisters.

Ⓒ Both narrators feel mocked and hated by their stepsisters.

Ⓓ Neither narrator wants her stepsisters to win the prince's heart.

Ⓔ Neither narrator expects her stepsisters to welcome her at the ball.

7. **Which character would you consider a role model, Cinderella or Cinder? Explain your choice.**

   _____

   _____

   _____

   _____

8. **What lesson, or theme, might readers learn from the poem and from the story? Write a theme for each work.**

   _____

   _____

   _____

   _____

   _____

   _____

English Language Arts

Cite Text Evidence to Support Inferences
Reading: Informational Text

DIRECTIONS: Read the passage. Then, answer the questions.

How Much Water?

[1] You hear lots of recommendations: Drink eight 8-ounce glasses of water every day! [2] Drink even more when it's hot outside! [3] Drink before, during, and after exercise. [4] Make sure the water's filtered. [5] Just drink it from the tap. [6] Who cares where the water comes from, as long as you drink a bunch? [7] Clearly, some of this advice contradicts other advice.

[8] So, who's right? [9] How much water should you drink for good health each day? [10] And, how much is too much? [11] Get the facts so you don't under- or overdo it. [12] You might be thinking, "Really? [13] People can drink too much water?" [14] A condition called hyponatremia results when people, usually endurance athletes, such as marathoners, drink so much water that the body's chemistry becomes imbalanced. [15] These people can become very sick.

[16] It's rare, however, that people drink too much water. [17] Usually, the opposite is the case: People don't get enough water each day, and they suffer from dehydration. [18] Even mild dehydration can cause headaches and fatigue. [19] Although expert advice differs slightly, the "eight-by-eight" rule is easy to remember and within the range of healthy water intake. [20] How much water a person needs depends, in fact, on how active the person is, whether the person is an adult or a child or a man or a woman, and the outside temperature.

[21] So, keep an eye on what's going on in your life each day. [22] If you sweat a lot, drink a bit more to offset the loss of water. Add a glass if you exercise vigorously. [23] Of course, any time you run a fever, your body loses water, so increase your fluid intake to compensate. [24] And, remember that other fluids, such as tea or juice, count in your fluid intake. [25] Cool, refreshing water is the best choice for optimal health and hydration, so make a habit of opting for water over sugar-laden soft drinks!

Strategy
Connect what you already know about the subjects you read about to the new information you learn from details. Combine the old and new information to draw a conclusion, or inference, about what you read.

Test Tip
Identify the purpose of an informational text to help you better understand why certain details are included.

1. **Which sentence from the passage supports the inference that the average reader is unlikely to suffer from hyponatremia?**

   (A) Sentence 23, because most readers are not running fevers

   (B) Sentence 14, because most readers are not endurance athletes

   (C) Sentence 18, because most readers experience headaches now and then

   (D) Sentence 13 because most readers doubt that people can drink too much water

Cite Text Evidence to Support Inferences
Reading: Informational Text

DIRECTIONS: Use the passage to choose or write the best answer.

> **Strategy** When looking for context clues, locate and mark words or phrases in the passage that may rename, explain, or define the word you don't know.

2. **Which sentence contains words that a writer could quote to support the inference that advice on how much water to drink is inconsistent and can be confusing? Choose two.**

   (A) Sentence 7

   (B) Sentence 15

   (C) Sentence 16

   (D) Sentence 19

   (E) Sentence 24

3. **Which word from the passage describes a physical condition and comes from a Latin prefix meaning "away from" or "down" and a Latin root meaning "water"?**

   (A) chemistry, in Sentence 14

   (B) dehydration, in Sentence 17

   (C) fatigue, in Sentence 18

   (D) optimal, in Sentence 25

   Write how you know.

   _____

   _____

   _____

   _____

   _____

4. **Which phrases in the context of the word *compensate* (sentence 23) suggest that to compensate means "to make up for" or "to account for"? Choose two.**

   (A) "if you exercise vigorously"

   (B) "body loses water"

   (C) "increase your fluid intake"

   (D) "other fluids, such as tea or juice, count"

   (E) "optimal health and hydration"

5. **A reader has made this inference after reading "How Much Water?": "The 'eight-by-eight rule' must refer to the recommendation that athletes should be careful not to drink too much water." Does the passage support this inference? Explain your answer.**

   _____

   _____

   _____

   _____

   _____

   _____

   _____

   _____

   _____

   _____

   _____

   _____

   _____

English Language Arts

Summarize Using Main Ideas and Details
Reading: Informational Text

DIRECTIONS: Read the passage. Then, answer the questions that follow.

Glorious Niagara

[1] Niagara Falls is one of the most spectacular natural wonders of the world. [2] Part of the Falls is in Ontario, Canada, and part is in New York State. [3] The Falls are supplied by the Niagara River, which connects Lake Ontario and Lake Erie. [4] The Niagara Falls are located midway in the river. [5] They pour 500,000 tons of water per minute into a deep gorge.

Formation of the Falls

[6] Geologists believe that Niagara Falls was formed after the last ice sheet from the Ice Age receded from the area. [7] The surface of the land was changed by the ice so that waterways and streams found new paths in which to flow. [8] One result was an overflow of Lake Erie approximately 20,000 years ago, creating Niagara Falls. [9] The Falls are formed over an outer layer of hard dolomitic limestone. [10] This covers a softer layer of shale. [11] The shale is more easily worn away, which causes the harder limestone to form an overhanging edge. [12] This allows the Falls to drop straight down at a sharp angle, which produces a spectacular sight.

[13] The outer layer has broken off at times over the years, causing the Falls to gradually move up the river. [14] This erosion is happening to the American Falls at the rate of 3–7 inches per year. [15] But, the edge of Horseshoe Falls is wearing away more quickly at a rate of about 3 feet per year.

Visitors to the Falls

[16] For many years, sightseers have traveled to Niagara Falls for the remarkable views from observation towers and the Cave of the Winds behind the Falls. [17] At night, lights flood the Falls. [18] A steamer called the *Maid of the Mist* takes visitors around the base of the falls, where they are both impressed and soaked by the roaring cascade.

[19] Niagara Falls has also irresistibly drawn daredevils who want to test their courage. [20] One such man, Charles Blondin, crossed the Falls on a tightrope in 1859 and repeated the feat 4 days later—this time blindfolded. [21] A month later, he carried a man on his shoulders as he crossed yet again. [22] As if that was not daring enough, Blondin returned for a fourth crossing—on stilts!

Strategy
To locate the main idea of a passage, look for the idea that appears in the introductory paragraph, is developed by other ideas in the body paragraph, and is repeated, perhaps in different words, in the conclusion paragraph.

Test Tip
Identify the main idea and important details in a passage. These are central ideas, or the most important ideas in the passage.

1. **Which statement best states the main idea of the entire passage?**

   (A) The end of the last Ice Age led to the formation of Niagara Falls.

   (B) Some people have traveled to Niagara Falls to take unnecessary risks.

   (C) Spectacular Niagara Falls formed long ago and draws many visitors to this day.

   (D) Visitors can view Niagara Falls from various places, including a cave behind the Falls.

English Language Arts

Summarize Using Main Ideas and Details
Reading: Informational Text

DIRECTIONS: Use the passage to choose or write the best answer.

Strategy

Summarize a passage using the most important ideas to show that you understand what you read.

Test Tip

When asked to summarize a passage, write the main idea in your own words first. Then, imagine that you are outlining the main points that support the main idea. Write these in your own words as well. Examples and explanations are not part of a summary, which contains only the main and supporting ideas. Improve your summary by including transitional words that link the main idea and supporting ideas logically.

2. **Part A: Why is Niagara Falls an ever-changing natural wonder, according to the passage?**

(A) Erosion causes the Falls to slowly shift upriver.

(B) The rate of flow over the Falls changes over time.

(C) The Falls draw different visitors with each passing year.

(D) The Falls look different when seen from the Cave of the Winds.

Part B: Which two sentences in the passage include details that support the answer to Part A?

(A) Sentence 5

(B) Sentence 8

(C) Sentence 11

(D) Sentence 13

(E) Sentence 18

3. **Review the last paragraph. What is the main reason the author lists Blondin's daring feats?**

(A) to prove that Blondin was brave and bold

(B) to give interesting facts about the history of the Falls

(C) to support the claim that the Falls attract thrill-seekers

(D) to warn readers against risky behavior like Blondin's actions

4. **Write a summary of the passage. Include the main ideas and transitions that link those ideas.**

Niagara Falls is an ever-changing wonder that has two falls. It also has the Maid of the Mist and the Cave of the winds. It attracts a lot of visitors.

Analyze Text Structure
Reading: Informational Text

DIRECTIONS: Read the passage. Then, answer the questions.

Ship of the Desert

Nomads who crisscross the Sahara, the great desert of North Africa, rely on a uniquely suited animal for transportation—the dromedary, or one-humped camel. Its ability to store fat, to conserve water, and to handle the desert environment makes it so indispensable to desert travel that the dromedary is sometimes called the ship of the desert.

Have Food, Will Travel

Several factors make the dromedary suitable for long desert trips. It can travel the sands for long periods without nourishment, an advantage where food must be carried. The hump on the camel's back serves as its food reserve. When it has little to eat, it converts the fat from its hump into energy. The camel's hump can weigh 80 pounds or more. When the animal has to rely on its reservoir of fat, the hump becomes much smaller. Thus, it is easy to recognize a well-fed camel by the size of its hump.

Water Tanks?

Many people believe that camels store water in their humps. This is not true. Their ability to go for days without drinking is due to other factors. First, camels are able to drink large quantities of water at one time. Some have been known to gulp 53 gallons in one day. Second, the camel sweats very little and can tolerate greater body temperatures than many animals can. Consequently, it retains most of the water it drinks and can travel several hundred miles before replenishing its supply.

Shielded from Sun and Sand

Other physical characteristics enable the camel to endure harsh desert conditions. It can completely close its nostrils, thus protecting it from the stinging effects of sandstorms. Its eyes are shielded from sand and sun by overhanging lids and long, thick lashes. In addition, its broad, padded feet keep it from sinking into the soft sand. No other animal is better equipped for life in the desert than the camel.

Strategy | Use a passage's structure to understand its main ideas.

Test Tip | Authors of informational articles often introduce the topics they will cover in the first paragraph. Look for sentences that give a preview of what the article will cover. Read the last sentence of the first paragraph. What topics will be covered in this passage?

1. According to the introduction, the author plans to discuss three advantages that the dromedary has for desert travel. Write the three advantages below.

   Stores tons of water, shielding from sun and sand, and has food ready.

How can you expect the rest of the passage to be organized?

The next part will explain the advantages more in detail.

English Language Arts

Analyze Text Structure
Reading: Informational Text

DIRECTIONS: Use the passage to choose or write the best answer.

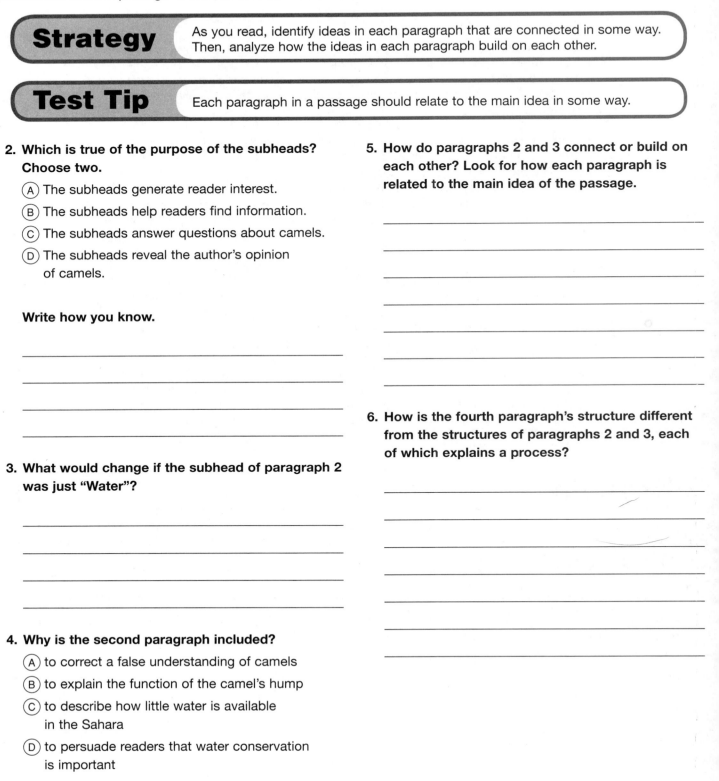

Strategy — As you read, identify ideas in each paragraph that are connected in some way. Then, analyze how the ideas in each paragraph build on each other.

Test Tip — Each paragraph in a passage should relate to the main idea in some way.

2. **Which is true of the purpose of the subheads? Choose two.**

   (A) The subheads generate reader interest.

   (B) The subheads help readers find information.

   (C) The subheads answer questions about camels.

   (D) The subheads reveal the author's opinion of camels.

   Write how you know.

   _____

   _____

   _____

   _____

3. **What would change if the subhead of paragraph 2 was just "Water"?**

   _____

   _____

   _____

   _____

4. **Why is the second paragraph included?**

   (A) to correct a false understanding of camels

   (B) to explain the function of the camel's hump

   (C) to describe how little water is available in the Sahara

   (D) to persuade readers that water conservation is important

5. **How do paragraphs 2 and 3 connect or build on each other? Look for how each paragraph is related to the main idea of the passage.**

   _____

   _____

   _____

   _____

   _____

   _____

   _____

6. **How is the fourth paragraph's structure different from the structures of paragraphs 2 and 3, each of which explains a process?**

   _____

   _____

   _____

   _____

   _____

   _____

Determine Author's Purpose
Reading: Informational Text

DIRECTIONS: Read the passage. Then, answer the questions.

[1] If you are learning to play the guitar, you might have reason to thank Nicholas Ravagni. [2] Ravagni owns a patent that helps new guitar players figure out where to place their fingers on the fingerboard. [3] Ravagni got the idea for his invention when he was only 6 and obtained his patent when he was 11. [4] He designed a self-adhesive, color-coded strip of plastic that fits under a guitar's strings and marks the right points to place fingers to play certain notes or chords.

[5] Ravagni is not the only young inventor who created helpful, everyday products. [6] If you open your refrigerator, you might find leftovers wrapped in aluminum foil. [7] Thank Charles Hall, a college student who experimented with a process to create a cheap and ready supply of aluminum. [8] When you tune into your favorite FM radio station, thank Edwin Armstrong. [9] Just after the turn of the 20th century, when he was only 15, Armstrong read a book about inventions and decided he would become an inventor of radios. [10] By the time he was in his early 20s, he made discoveries that would lead to his development of the FM radio.

Strategy

When you read to determine the author's purpose, keep the most common purposes for writing informational text in mind. Ask: *What does the author hope readers will do with the information presented?*

Test Tip

Know the most common purposes for informational texts:
- To satisfy reader curiosity about how or why something happens
- To instruct or teach readers how to do something
- To persuade readers to consider an idea or take action

1. **Part A: What attitude toward young inventors does the writer want readers to have?**

   ● envious
   Ⓑ doubtful
   ● grateful
   Ⓓ surprised

Part B: Write a sentence from the passage that supports your answer to Part A.

The author wants us to follow big dreams as kids and then to follow them when older.

English Language Arts

Determine Author's Purpose

Reading: Informational Text

DIRECTIONS: Use the passage to choose or write the best answer.

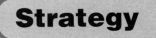 **Strategy** — Identify words, phrases, or sentences in the passage that tell how the author thinks or feels about the topic.

2. **Which choice describes the author's main purpose for writing this passage?**

   (A) to inform readers about young inventors

   (B) to explain how to obtain a patent

   (C) to persuade readers to buy Ravagni's invention

   (D) to advise readers to learn to play an instrument

3. **Besides the main purpose, the author may also hope to influence young readers to act in a certain way. In your own words, explain the action young readers might be inspired to take after reading the article.**

   _____

   _____

   _____

4. **What does the author think or feel about Ravagni? Explain your answer.**

   _____

   _____

   _____

   _____

   _____

   _____

5. **Why does the author give several examples of young inventors rather than writing only about Nicholas Ravagni?**

   (A) to explain how to get an idea for an invention

   (B) to identify problems that new inventions might solve

   (C) to encourage readers to read about other young inventors

   (D) to support the idea that young people can succeed at inventing

   Write how you know.

   _____

   _____

   _____

   _____

   _____

   _____

   _____

   _____

   _____

6. **The author writes about the success of young inventors. How would the passage be different if it only included information about Ravagni?**

   _____

   _____

   _____

   _____

Evaluate Arguments
Reading: Informational Text

DIRECTIONS: Read the passage. Then, answer the questions.

Strategy — Identify an author's claim, or position, about the topic. Then, reread the passage to determine if the author has included enough details to support the position or claim.

Pitch the Plastic

[1] They're convenient. [2] They're attractive. [3] And they're everywhere. [4] They're plastic, single-serve water bottles. [5] Almost everyone uses them from time to time; some people use them every day. [6] People buy them at grocery stores and gas stations, stow them in coolers and backpacks, use them once, and then toss them out. [7] And therein lies the problem: Single-serve water bottles are a huge—and utterly unnecessary—source of land and ocean pollution today.

[8] Some people would deny that single-serve plastic bottles are a problem, but that's because they don't like the taste of tap water. [9] In my opinion, tap water tastes just fine, and there's no good reason to pay for water that's been trucked in from some place else. [10] But, personal taste preferences aside, there are valid reasons to quit using single-serve plastic bottles.

[11] Pollution: It is true that most single-serve bottles can be recycled, so buyers who insist on using plastic should at least check the recycling code on the bottle. [12] A code 1 or 2 is most recyclable, and a code 5 or 6 is less so. [13] But, even people with good intentions may fail to recycle. [14] Some estimates suggest that only 1 plastic bottle out of 6 is recycled. [15] Worse still, even those bottles that are recycled will often end up in landfills in their recycled form at some point because plastics degrade during recycling. [16] Also, what about those bottles not recycled? [17] They litter our land and float into the oceans, where the currents gather them into enormous gyres of trash, like floating islands of plastic. [18] Some plastics eventually break into smaller pieces that fish and birds mistake for food; when they eat the plastic, they often become ill or die. [19] It's quite difficult to properly dispose of plastic in a way that does no harm to the environment.

[20] Costs: Plastics are petroleum products. [21] Yes, the same oil that becomes gasoline for our cars also becomes plastic bottles. [22] That petroleum must be acquired, at a high cost, from under the ground or ocean. It must then must be refined and trucked to manufacturing facilities. Once the bottles are made, they use more highway or rail miles to get to stores. [23] In addition, various chemicals are added to the plastic to produce the right balance of flexibility and sturdiness, and there is some evidence that these chemicals may be health hazards.

[24] Convenience and usability are not strong enough reasons to continue relying on single-serve plastic bottles. [25] Some cities have already acknowledged the problems and are in the process of phasing out single-serve plastic bottles, but individuals do not need to wait for cities to act. [26] All that's required is that individuals purchase a sturdy bottle that can be filled, washed, and refilled for years—a simple solution to a complex problem.

1. Write the topic of the passage.

Save our World from Plastic

Write how you know.

The passage had many reason to quit using plastic around the globe.

Evaluate Arguments
Reading: Informational Text

DIRECTIONS: Use the passage to choose or write the best answer.

> **Test Tip** A claim is an opinion or idea that an author has about a topic. A position is the side the author takes on a controversial issue.

2. **What technique does the author use to introduce the topic in the first paragraph? Choose three.**

   (A) She describes the pollution caused by plastic bottles.

   (B) She grabs the reader's attention with short, parallel sentences.

   (C) She creates suspense, not telling the reader until Sentence 4 to find out what "they" are.

   (D) She appeals to the reader's desire to save money and help the environment.

   (E) She presents what sounds like a good thing and then suddenly announces it is a bad thing.

3. **Part A: Which statement accurately summarizes the author's claim about why so many people use single-serve plastic bottles?**

   (A) People intend to recycle all the bottles they use.

   (B) People are not aware of the real cost of these bottles.

   (C) People do not mind paying extra to have water in these bottles.

   (D) People think the water in these bottles tastes better than tap water.

Part B: What type of evidence is used to support this claim?

(A) the author's personal tastes

(B) scientific research into water quality

(C) taste tests of bottled water and tap water

(D) industry research on the market for bottled water

Part C: Why is the author's explanation in the second paragraph about why people choose single-serve plastic bottles an example of a weak argument and evidence?

_____

_____

_____

_____

_____

_____

_____

_____

Evaluate Arguments
Reading: Informational Text

DIRECTIONS: Use the passage to choose or write the best answer.

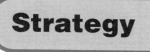 Mark the passage as you read, looking for evidence to support the claim. Use question marks to mark evidence you find doubtful, and use stars to mark evidence you find convincing.

4. **What evidence does the author give that recycling is not an adequate solution to the plastic-bottle problem? Choose two.**

   (A) Most plastic bottles are simply thrown away.

   (B) Some cities have decided to ban plastic bottles.

   (B) Bits of plastic bottles can kill fish and sea birds.

   (D) Plastic degrades when it is made into something else.

Test Tip

Check the credibility of an author's sources by thinking about who did the research the author cites. Were the researchers unbiased, seeking only the facts and not thinking about how the research might help them make money? Or, were they looking for information to support their own position? Unbiased research is more credible than research done to support a position or help a business make more money.

5. **The author checked several sources to get information about the costs of plastic production. Read the information about each source. For each source, write "likely unbiased, more credible" or "possibly biased, less credible" on the line.**

First source: a report on petroleum costs written by a major oil producer and refiner

_____

_____

Second source: a government-funded study of costs to repair highways and rail lines used to move manufactured goods to stores

_____

_____

Third source: an interview with the manager of a factory where reusable metal bottles are made

_____

_____

6. **Which of the three sources in question 5 is the least credible? Explain your reasoning.**

_____

_____

_____

_____

_____

_____

_____

_____

_____

7. **If you wanted to find additional evidence to support the claim that plastic bottles are a major source of ocean pollution, which source would likely provide unbiased, credible evidence? Choose two.**

   (A) a blog on ocean travel written by a world traveler

   (B) photographs and maps showing plastic islands in the oceans

   (c) personal stories of a friend who cleans up plastic trash along the shoreline

   (D) an article by a wildlife biologist who has found plastic bits in dead sea birds' stomachs

Evaluate Arguments
Reading: Informational Text

DIRECTIONS: Use the passage and the chart to choose or write the best answer.

Strategy Use information presented in visuals such as charts, tables, graphs, photos, and drawings. Compare the information in the visuals to the details in the text.

Test Tip Read all of the parts of charts, tables, and diagrams to make sure you understand the information presented. Read titles, captions, labels, and numbers.

8. The title of this chart is "Single-Serve vs. Reusable—An Easy Choice." Next to each entry in the chart, write a check mark if the author would agree that the entry describes a positive trait and an X if the author would agree that the entry describes a negative trait. Then, answer the question.

Single-Serve Plastic Bottle	Reusable Bottle
unbreakable	unbreakable
must be thrown away or recycled after one use	can be washed and reused many times
must purchase a new bottle for every drink	must purchase only once
may leach tiny amounts of dangerous chemicals	chemical-free
can hold only cold or room temperature liquids	metal varieties can hold hot or cold liquids
greater manufacturing and transportation costs if used often	one-time manufacturing and transportation costs

How does this chart support the author's purpose in the passage?

_____

_____

_____

_____

9. **Do you agree with the author's claim or position? Explain your answer.**

_____

_____

_____

_____

English Language Arts

Determine the Meanings of Words and Phrases
Language

DIRECTIONS: Each excerpt that follows is from the same informational article. Read each excerpt. Then, answer the questions that follow.

Tools for Tight Spots

   Here's an interesting scene: Archaeologists have discovered an ancient tomb. Of course, they want to know what's inside, but if they open the tomb too quickly, they might damage the artifacts. They need to send something in through a narrow crack to investigate. Origami robots to the rescue! Teams of university researchers are collaborating to create tiny robots that are thin and flat, like a sheet of thick paper. Origami, the Japanese art of paper folding, provides techniques to fold robotic parts into small packages that researchers can then unfold and use. Until now, however, folded robots have required people to unfold and reactivate them.

Strategy When you encounter an unfamiliar word, look nearby for these context clues: synonyms or phrases that rename the word, antonyms, examples of the thing the word names, and descriptions of things the word names.

Test Tip Not only word roots, but also word prefixes and suffixes can help you figure out the meaning of unfamiliar words. Learn basic prefix meanings: *re-* (again), *dis-* (bad, ill), *pre-* (before), *co-*, *com-*, and *col-* (together), and *inter-* (between). Use the Internet to find prefixes and suffixes, and learn a few each week.

1. **Part A: Context clues such as "Teams" and "create" and the meaning of the prefix and root in** *collaborating* **help readers determine that the word means _____**

   (A) doing research

   (B) studying robots

   (C) assembling parts

   (D) working together

   Part B: Write the prefix and root in the word *collaborating* **and their meanings.**

   _____

   _____

2. **What do the root and prefix in** *reactivate* **mean?**

   _____

   _____

Rewrite the last sentence, using your definition of *reactivate*.

   _____

   _____

   _____

   _____

3. **How do root words, prefixes, and suffixes help you understand unknown words?**

   _____

   _____

   _____

   _____

Determine the Meanings of Words and Phrases
Language

DIRECTIONS: Read the excerpt from an informational article. Then, answer the questions.

Strategy Determine the meaning of an unknown word by using the words and phrases near the unknown word.

Test Tip Try out different meanings in a sentence to see which one makes sense.

The robots are constructed from sheets of thick paper, thin circuit boards, and joints made from pre-stretched polystyrene, a material that, when heated, contracts to tighten the robot's joints into the correct angles, pulling the folded pieces up and together. The unfolded robot also has tiny motors, so once the polystyrene joints cool and harden, the robot can walk to its programmed destination.

Researchers predict these tiny robots will be functional in places people can't easily go: into space as miniscule satellites, onto the inhospitable surface of Mars to explore, or into the ruins of collapsed buildings to assist in search and rescue operations.

4. **Which context clues in the first paragraph clarify the meaning of *contracts*? Choose two.**

   (A) constructed of sheets

   (B) polystyrene, a material

   (C) to tighten the robot's joints

   (D) pulling the folded pieces up and together

   Write a definition of *contracts* based on these context clues.

   _____

   _____

5. **What does "functional" mean, given the three examples of functional robots provided in the second paragraph—"as miniscule satellites," "to explore," and "to assist in search and rescue operations"?**

   (A) foldable

   (B) challenging

   (C) unreachable

   (D) useful

Write how you know.

   _____

   _____

   _____

   _____

   _____

   _____

   _____

6. **The prefix *mini-* means "small." What word in the second paragraph is a synonym for "miniscule"?**

   _____

English Language Arts

Understand Word Relationships
Language

DIRECTIONS: Read each excerpt. Then, answer the questions.

> The natural world is the stage for many exciting and physically challenging activities. Those who live on the edge of the continent can sail, swim, and surf. Skiers and hikers love the mountains, whereas rivers attract those who love to fish, canoe, and raft. Yet, nature can also be a dangerous playmate for those who come unprepared for the challenge.

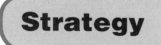 **Strategy** — Look at details, contexts of the same sentence and near the unfamiliar word, and word clues such as word parts (roots, prefixes, and affixes) to understand how words are related in a passage.

1. Which figure of speech is used to describe nature in the last sentence?

- (A) exaggeration
- (B) metaphor
- (C) personification
- (D) simile

What is the purpose of the figure of speech in the passage?

_____
_____
_____
_____

2. How is the natural world a stage as described in the passage?

_____
_____
_____
_____
_____
_____
_____
_____

> What makes a person prepared to enjoy the natural world safely? Prepared people know their limits: for example, how long they can stay out in hot or cold weather, how much water they should carry with them, and of course, how to keep an eye on changing conditions. Unwary people, on the other hand, can quickly find themselves in trouble.

3. Which phrase tells readers that *unwary* means the opposite of prepared and helps them understand the less familiar word?

- (A) on the other hand
- (B) for example
- (C) of course
- (D) to enjoy

4. Write the words and phrases that you can use to help determine the meaning of the phrase "know their limits" as used in the passage.

_____
_____
_____
_____
_____

Name _____ Date 10-11-19

English Language Arts

Understand Word Relationships
Language

DIRECTIONS: Read each excerpt. Then, answer the questions.

Strategy Use context to determine if words and phrases have literal meanings—dictionary definitions—or nonliteral meanings—figurative language.

Climbers tackle two kinds of problems. Bouldering requires climbers to grip the rock face with their hands and feet to climb short distances. If they fall, they land on thick "crash pads" at the base of the boulder. Sport climbers scale tall rock faces and must be attached to ropes at all times. One climber climbs while another stands at the base of the rock to keep the ropes taut. Sport climbing requires more stamina than bouldering.

5. **Which definition of the word *tackle* is most likely correct in this context?**

   (A) begin
   (B) equipment
   (C) knock down by force
   (D) undertake the challenge

Test Tip

Idioms are one kind of figurative language. An idiom cannot be taken literally: "The doting grandparents wanted to give the grandchild the moon" does not mean that anyone can give the moon as a gift. The idiom means that the grandparents love the grandchild deeply and will do what they can to keep the grandchild happy. When you read, look for idioms and decide what idea they communicate.

When climbers find a bouldering route that is both challenging and cleverly laid out, they say the route is "sick" or "rad." They might call out "beta," or advice, to someone trying to complete the climb: "Left foot down to that ledge" or "Grip the crack with your right hand." When a climber "sends" a difficult route, or completes it on the first try, she has really set the world on fire.

6. **The last sentence of the passage has the idiom "she has really set the world on fire." What does this idiom literally mean?** Did the thing amazingly.

(A) She feels a sense of accomplishment.
(B) She feels hot and tired after her efforts.
(C) She feels relief to have finished the climb.
(D) She feels grateful for the advice other climbers gave her.

Strategy

Use what you know about root words to figure out the meaning of unfamiliar words.

Test Tip

Search the Internet for a list of root words and their meanings. Study a new root each week to build your knowledge of roots.

Some words have more than one root you can use to determine the meaning. The root word *bene-* means "good" or "well," and the root word *fic-* means "do" or "make." Both roots are in the word *beneficial*.

7. **What kind of exercise would be *beneficial* for someone who wants to climb rock faces? Explain your answer.**

Mountain Climbers because you are "climbing" and it gives you more grip.

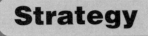

English Language Arts

Write an Argument
Writing

Strategy   When you are asked to write an argument, state a claim about the subject you choose or are assigned. Then, support your claim with evidence: facts, reasons, explanations, and expert opinions.

Test Tip   An argument is more convincing if you consider evidence others might offer against your claim. Acknowledge this evidence, and then, show why it is not useful, true, or correct.

DIRECTIONS: Choose a topic that reasonable people might disagree on. You might argue that your community needs to take action on water conservation or that young people should have greater access to afterschool programs and activities. Then, complete the organizer by writing your answers for each step in the space provided.

STEP 1: State your claim.

My claim:

STEP 2: Consider the evidence.

Evidence for my claim	Evidence others might offer against my claim:

STEP 3: Organize your evidence logically. For example, you might use time order, cause-effect order, or order of importance. Begin each item on your list with transition words, such as *first or most important.*

1.

2.

3.

STEP 4: Write a conclusion that sums up what you want your reader to do or to remember.

My conclusion:

Write an Argument
Writing

DIRECTIONS: Read the passage. Then, answer the questions that follow.

[1] City planner Hannah Green recently warned that households that water lawns during the heat of the day will receive a fine. [2] "We must do something," Ms. Green said, "to stop the waste of midday watering." [3] Ms. Green cited studies that show that a significant percentage of water evaporates in the hot sunshine before it can reach the roots of thirsty plants. [4] Think about it, people—doesn't it make sense to water when it's cool and dark? [5] Some people object to getting up to water at night. [6] However, households with sprinkler systems can easily program them to start just before sunrise. [7] In addition, watering early in the morning is an option.

1. **What evidence does Ms. Green offer for why people should not water during the heat of the day?**
   - (A) People who water midday will be fined.
   - (B) The city is running short on water supplies.
   - (C) Only some households have sprinkler systems.
   - (D) Studies show that water is lost to the hot air.

2. **Rewrite Sentence 4 so it matches the formal tone of the rest of the passage. Use a transition that shows how your new sentence is related to Sentence 3.**

   _____

   _____

   _____

   _____

   _____

   _____

3. **Write a conclusion to an argument paper on responsible lawn watering. If you agree with the writer of the article and Ms. Green, that midday watering must stop, you may write a conclusion for the passage. If you disagree with the passage, write a conclusion that expresses your point of view on responsible lawn watering.**

   _____

   _____

   _____

   _____

   _____

   _____

   _____

Name _____ Date 10-22-19

English Language Arts

Write an Informative Text
Writing

DIRECTIONS: Read the passage from a student's informative essay. Then, answer the questions.

> On April 14, 1865, citizens in Washington, D.C., were in the mood to celebrate. The long and terrible war was over, and President Abraham Lincoln had just spoken to crowds about how the nation could begin to heal "with malice toward none, with charity for all." April 14th found President and Mrs. Lincoln at the theater watching a comedy. Mary Todd Lincoln later said that her husband was more relaxed and happy than he had been in years. However, this peaceful moment was shattered when, a little after 10 o'clock, a handsome actor named John Wilkes Booth slipped into the president's box and shot him at close range. Lincoln died early the next morning. Booth assassinated Lincoln because Booth hated the Union, and he hoped that if Lincoln and other government leaders died, the Confederacy would start the war again. You can bet that Booth and his partners in crime were hunted and nabbed!

Strategy

As you plan your writing, choose a text structure that fits the information you want to communicate.

Test Tip

Possible structures include:
- explain a problem and offer a solution (problem-solution)
- explain how some events caused others (cause-effect)
- explain events that happened over time (time order or chronology)
- explain how things are alike and unalike (comparison-contrast)
- explain what a thing is like (definition)

1. **What structure did the student use to organize this introductory paragraph?**

   (A) definition

   (B) time order

   (C) compare-contrast

   (D) order of importance

2. **Write the sentence in which the student used a transition word to signify a cause-effect relationship between events in the paragraph.**

   Booth assassinated Lincoln because Booth hated the Union, and he hoped that if Lincoln and other government leaders died, the Confederacy would start the war again.

3. **Most of the language the student uses is formal. How would you rewrite the final sentence to replace the informal expression with more formal language?**

   Booth and his partners were probably hurt and harmed after what they did.

Write an Informative Text
Writing

4. Why did the student include quoted words from the speech Lincoln made after the Civil War ended?

_____

_____

_____

_____

5. If the student wanted more information about the assassination of President Lincoln, which three search terms would return the most information? Choose the best three answers.

Ⓐ famous actors

Ⓑ Abraham Lincoln

Ⓒ Washington, D. C.

Ⓓ John Wilkes Booth

Ⓔ United States history

Ⓕ newspaper headlines April 15, 1865

6. Part A: A search for "Abraham Lincoln facts" returned lists of facts from several sources. Which source is most likely a credible source for information about Lincoln's service as president during the Civil War?

Ⓐ TourDCwithUs.com

Ⓑ Lincoln: Boyhood Stories

Ⓒ "Divided We Fall": Lincoln and a Nation in Crisis

Ⓓ Lincoln on Stage: Actors Who Have Played Lincoln

Part B: Explain your answer to Part A.

_____

_____

_____

_____

_____

_____

_____

_____

_____

_____

Test Tip

When you paraphrase a source, use your own words to communicate the information in the sentences you sum up. If you use the source's words, you must put them in quotation marks. Otherwise, you are plagiarizing—pretending that you wrote something that another writer wrote.

7. A student read the following in a source:

The Library of Congress—America's Story website has this comment on the assassination: "Why did Booth do it? He thought it would aid the South, which had just surrendered to Federal forces. It had nearly the opposite effect, ending Lincoln's plans for a rather generous peace."

The student paraphrased the quotation this way:

According to the Library of Congress, Booth thought the assassination would aid the South, which had just lost the war, but in fact, Lincoln's death made things worse for the South.

Explain two ways in which this sentence fails to paraphrase the Library of Congress source correctly.

_____

_____

_____

_____

_____

Write an Informative Text
Writing

> ## Strategy
> When you paraphrase, be sure to capture each idea in the source.

8. The following quotation is from a source about Abraham Lincoln:

Many historians argue that if Lincoln had lived to serve a second term as president, the southern states would come back into the nation on kinder terms. However, after Lincoln's death, some Union states wanted to punish the South—for the war, for all of their losses, and for Lincoln's demise. The harsh demands and treatment of the southern states did little to relieve the anger between former Union and Confederate states.

How might this quotation be paraphrased? Remember that any words you take directly from the source must be placed in quotation marks, except for technical terms.

_____

_____

_____

_____

_____

_____

_____

_____

_____

_____

> ## Test Tip
> Follow the correct format when you list sources you used for research. MLA style is often used to cite sources. You can get help with MLA style from Purdue OWL or Citation Machine.

This is an example of how to cite a book using MLA style. "Medium of Publication" means whether the book was published by printing and binding, by posting it online, or in another electronic format.

Author's last name, author's first name. *Title of Book*. City of Publication: Publisher, Year of Publication. Medium of Publication.

Hamilton, Edith. *Mythology*. Boston: Little, Brown and Company, 1942. Print.

9. Create an MLA-style citation for this source:

Book name: *Chasing Lincoln's Killer*

Author: James Swanson

Publisher: Scholastic Press

Medium of Publication: Print

City of Publication: New York

Date of Publication: 2009

_____

_____

_____

Name _____ Date _____

Write an Informative Text
Writing

DIRECTIONS: Write three paragraphs about the assassination of Lincoln or another historical event. Include the following:

- Information from at least two sources
- Facts about the event
- A claim about why the event is important
- An explanation of what happened during the event
- Names of people who played important roles in the event
- A correctly formatted list of the sources you used at the end

Plan your informative article by looking up at least two sources on your topic. Then, choose an organizational plan. Writers often use time order when they inform readers about an event, but cause-effect order is also useful. Use your organizational plan to place your notes in order.

_____

_____

_____

_____

_____

_____

_____

_____

_____

_____

_____

_____

_____

_____

_____

English Language Arts

Write a Narrative
Writing

DIRECTIONS: Read the story. Then, answer the questions.

> [1] Drew grabbed one end of the book, but Dan had a firm grip on the other as both pulled hard. [2] "It's my copy," Drew yelled, "so let go!" [3] Dan protested through gritted teeth that he had already read half the book and wanted to finish it that day. [4] The book slipped out of Drew's hands, and Dan fell backward onto the couch. [5] "What is going on here?" Dad said, glancing into the room from the hallway. [6] "We both want to read the latest novel in the series we've been following, but we've got just one book—and it's mine!" Drew insisted. [7] Dad frowned as Drew made another grab for the book. [8] "Hold on, guys. There's a better way to handle this problem," Dad said calmly.

Strategy Bring your characters to life by including details about how they move, how they look, and what they think and feel.

Test Tip One way to plan a story is to answer these questions about your main characters: *What do they want or need? What is stopping them from getting what they want or need? How do they finally get what they want or need?*

1. **What two tasks does the writer achieve in sentence 1?**

   (A) She reveals who will win the struggle.

   (B) She establishes the story's point of view.

   (C) She introduces the main characters and their conflict.

   (D) She explains how the main characters know each other.

2. **Which phrase could be added to sentence 4 to create a better connection with sentence 3?**

   (A) In fact,

   (B) Luckily,

   (C) After all,

   (D) Suddenly,

Strategy
Use details that appeal to the senses—sight, hearing, touch, taste, and smell.

3. **Rewrite Sentence 4 so that it includes descriptive details.**

   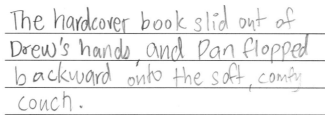
   The hardcover book slid out of Drew's hands, and Dan flopped backward onto the soft, comfy couch.

4. **Sentence 3 summarizes Dan's reply to Drew. Rewrite sentence 3 so that Dan, not the narrator, gives his reason for wanting the book.**

   Dan demanded yelling, " I already finished half the book and I want to read it now!".

English Language Arts

Write a Narrative
Writing

DIRECTIONS: A narrative is a story that tells about real or imagined events. Write a narrative about an invention that has made your life easier. It can be a real invention or one you make up. Write your paragraph on the lines. Your paragraph should have the following:

- A narrator and/or characters
- A natural sequence of events
- Dialogue
- Descriptions of actions, thoughts, and feelings
- Time words and phrases to show the order of events
- Concrete words and sensory details
- A sentence to end your paragraph

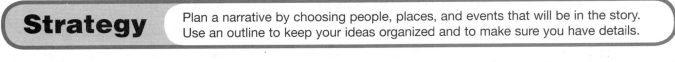

Strategy   Plan a narrative by choosing people, places, and events that will be in the story. Use an outline to keep your ideas organized and to make sure you have details.

Test Tip   Make sure the events in your narrative are organized and follow a clear order.

_____

_____

_____

_____

_____

_____

_____

_____

_____

_____

_____

Understand Editing and Revising
Writing

DIRECTIONS: Read the article. Then, answer the questions.

Counting, Inca Style

[1] You can count on fingers and toes, you can count with tally marks, or, if you lived in the Incan city of Cuzco in the 15th century or so, you could count with nots. [2] The people in the Incan city had an interesting way of keeping track of measurements, goods, and other things that needed to be counted and recorded. [3] They created *khipu* cords in which knots were tied to represent numbers and amounts. [4] The cords could be made of twisted fabric leather thongs or even animal hair. [5] *Khipu* theirselves, consisted of a series of cords hanging side by side. [6] When them are bundled up, *khipu* look a little like tangled mops. [7] However anyone who could read the cords could make their living keeping records and even encoding messages. [8] Different colors of cords stood for different metals—yellow cords for gold, for example. [9] Different kinds of knots stood for units like 5s and 10s. [10] About 600 *khipu* have survived the centuries since there use. [11] Many in museums.

Strategy   Revise your writing before you edit. Revision changes content, so if you edit before revising, you will need to edit again after revising to check the new content.

Test Tip   Don't worry about spelling and punctuation when you revise. You can find and fix those errors when you edit.

1. **Which revision corrects the pronoun error in Sentence 5?**

   A) *Khipu*, itself, consisted of a series of cords hanging side by side.

   B) *Khipu*, themselves, consisted of a series of cords hanging side by side.

   C) *Khipu*, their selves, consisted of a series of cords hanging side by side.

   D) *Khipu* theirselves consisted of a series of cords hanging side by side.

2. **Sentence 3 begins with an unclear pronoun. Which word correctly replaces the vague pronoun and adds specific meaning to the sentence?**

   A) Incans

   B) Knots

   C) People

   D) You

3. **Which word should be spelled differently?**

   A) since (Sentence 10)

   B) nots (Sentence 1)

   C) tied (Sentence 3)

   D) records (Sentence 7)

   Write the correct spelling of the word you chose.

   knots

4. **A pronoun can be used to replace the noun in Sentence 2. Rewrite the sentence using the correct pronoun.**

   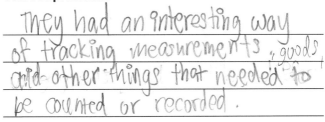
   They had an interesting way of tracking measurements, goods, and other things that needed to be counted or recorded.

Editing and Revising
Writing

5. Sentence 7 has a shift in pronoun number. Which revision uses both pronouns correctly?

(A) However, anyone who could read the cords could make their living keeping records and even recording messages.

(B) However, anyone who could read the cords could make his or her living keeping records and even recording messages.

(C) However, everybody who could read the cords could make their living keeping records and even recording messages.

(D) However, someone who could read the cords could make our living keeping records and even recording messages.

6. Sentence 6 uses a pronoun in the wrong case. Rewrite the sentence so that the pronoun is correct.

_____

_____

7. Where should a comma be added to Sentence 4?

(A) between *twisted* and *fabric*

(B) between *fabric* and *leather*

(C) between *leather* and *thongs*

(D) between *animal* and *hair*

8. Where should a comma be added to Sentence 3?

(A) between *khipu* and *cords*

(B) between *which* and *knots*

(C) between *represent* and *numbers*

(D) between *and* and *amounts*

9. Which word should be spelled differently?

(A) fabric (Sentence 4)

(B) series (Sentence 5)

(C) encoding (Sentence 7)

(D) there (Sentence 10)

10. Where should a comma be added to Sentence 7?

(A) between *keeping* and *records*

(B) between *who* and *could*

(C) between *However* and *anyone*

(D) between *read* and *the*

11. Which sentence is a fragment?

_____

Rewrite the fragment so that it is a complete sentence.

_____

_____

_____

_____

Name _____ Date _____

English Language Arts

Strategy Review

DIRECTIONS: Each strategy below is followed by a review, a passage, and one or more questions. Use these to review important strategies.

Read the story. Then, answer the questions.

> **Donkey for Sale**
> A man wished to purchase a donkey and agreed with its owner that he should test the animal before he bought him. He took the donkey home and put him in the straw yard with his other donkeys, upon which the new animal left all of the others and, at once, joined the one that was most idle and the greatest eater of them all. Seeing this, the man put a halter on the donkey and led him back to his owner. On being asked how, in so short a time, he could have made a trial of him, he answered, "I do not need a trial; I know that he will be just the same as the one he chose for his companion."

Strategy Use details from the text to make inferences, understand theme, and determine meaning.

What is a theme? In fiction, a theme can be one of the following:
- a lesson learned by characters or the reader
- an observation about how people often behave
- a general idea about the world and life

Writers rarely state a theme outright. Instead, they include details in the story to help readers find the theme on their own. When you have found a story's theme, you can state it in your own words.

1. **"Donkey for Sale" is a fable, a little story with a lesson to be learned. In your own words, write the lesson, which is the story's theme.**

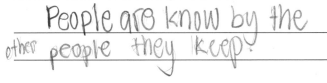 People are know by the other people they keep.

Strategy

Identify literary or structural elements, and use them to understand the meaning of a text.

Read the beginning of "The Echoing Green," by William Blake.

> The sun does arise,
> And make happy the skies.
> The merry bells ring
> To welcome the spring.
> The skylark and thrush,
> The birds of the bush,
> Sing louder around,
> To the bells' cheerful sound,
> While our sports shall be seen
> On the echoing green.

A *genre* is a type of literature, such as poetry or drama. Recognizing genres helps you understand how to interpret a poem, story, drama, or nonfiction article.

2. **How can you tell that "The Echoing Green" is a poem? Choose two answers.**

Ⓐ The speakers are children.

Ⓑ Rhyming words follow a pattern.

Ⓒ The lines follow a pattern of rhythm.

Ⓓ Skies cannot really be happy or unhappy.

Ⓔ The lines mention natural things like birds.

Ⓕ The language is figurative rather than literal.

English Language Arts

Strategy Review

> **The Texas Famine**
> *Clara Barton, nurse and Red Cross organizer, writes about a crisis that required Red Cross aid.*
>
> Before the close of the following year, 1885, came what was known as the "Texas Famine." Thousands of miles of wild land, forming the Panhandle, had been suddenly opened by the building of a Southern Railroad. In the speculative anxiety of the Road to people its newly acquired territory, unwarranted inducements of climatic advantages[1] had been unscrupulously held out to the poor farmers of Mississippi, Alabama, and Georgia.
>
> Lured by the pictures presented to them, some thousands of families had been induced to leave their old, worn-out farms, and with the little they could carry or drive, reach the new Eldorado[2], to find a new farm that needed only the planting to make them rich, prosperous, and happy, without labor. They planted.
>
> [1] "unwarranted inducements of climatic advantages": lies about how good the weather was for farming, told by people who wanted settlers to come to the Texas Panhandle
>
> [2] "Eldorado": a fabled land where all is made of precious gold and jewels

Strategy Reread texts to make comparisons, draw conclusions, or support inferences.

1. **Part A: What can readers infer about Clara Barton's opinion of the Southern Railroad agents who invited farmers to the Texas Panhandle?**

   (A) She considers them good businessmen.

   (B) She finds their actions dishonest and cruel.

   (C) She is glad that they helped the people during the famine.

   (D) She understands why they wanted people to farm near the rail lines.

   Part B: Cite a detail from the excerpt that supports your answer to Part A.

   She might think this way because lots of Southern families were forced to move to Eldorado.

English Language Arts

Strategy Review

Strategy — Use word clues in a text to identify its structure, to see how ideas in a text are related, and to clarify word meanings.

Here, Barton describes what happened to the Texas panhandle farmers.

The first year brought some returns—the second was a drought with no returns—the third the same. Hunger for themselves and starvation for their stock stared them in the face. They could not pick up and go back—the rivers were dry from the Rio Grande to the Brazos—the earth was iron, and the heavens brass; cattle wandered at will for water and feed, and their bones whitened the plains.

These were poor little peoples. They tried to make the great State know of their distress, but the rich railroad proprietors held the press, and no one knew their condition or could get correct information. At length a faithful clergyman came to Washington, to President Cleveland, and the Red Cross.

We consulted with the President, who gave encouragement for us to go to Texas and learn the facts.

Context clues are words or phrases within a passage that help you understand unfamiliar words. You can find hints about a word's meaning in the sentence in which it occurs and in nearby sentences:

The unscrupulous agents lied about the land's farming possibilities, tricking the people into moving to the panhandle.

You may not know what *unscrupulous* means, but you probably know what lying and tricking are and why they are wrong. So, you can guess that unscrupulous people are people willing to lie and trick others to get what they want.

3. **Write the information from the passage that helps you find the meaning of the word *stock* in the clause "starvation for their stock stared them in the face."**

   _____

   _____

   _____

   _____

   _____

Transitions are words or phrases that show how ideas are connected. Words like *before, following,* or *at last* can signal how events are related in time. Transitions like *because* or *as a result* can show a cause-effect relationship. An Internet search for "transition words" will provide lists of more transition words or phrases.

2. **Write a phrase from the passage that identifies the moment when the people could first hope for a solution to their problems. Explain why you chose this phrase.**

   _____

   _____

   _____

   _____

   _____

Strategy Review

> Born in 1888, Huddie Ledbetter, nicknamed "Leadbelly," was a blues guitarist who inspired generations of musicians. For much of his life, he wandered from place to place, playing anywhere he could. In 1934, he was discovered by John and Alan Lomax, who helped him find a larger audience for his music. Soon, he was playing in colleges, clubs, and music halls. He was featured on radio and television shows. Leadbelly died in 1949, but his music lives on. Musicians in many styles credit him with laying the foundation for today's popular music.

Details can be either helpful or distracting. The writer of this passage knows that some readers will not know much about the history of blues music. He can add details to explain blues music, but he must be careful to stay on topic. Even an interesting idea may distract readers if it is off topic.

Strategy When writing, use details to support, explain, or clarify your main ideas.

1. **Which details could the writer add to the passage to clarify what blues music is without distracting readers from the main idea of the paragraph?**

   (A) Some people like to dance to blues music.

   (B) Blues music gave rise to some types of American jazz.

   (C) Blind Willie Johnson was a blues musician from Texas.

   (D) Blues music began when field workers sang to pass the time.

2. **Write two sentences that give details about how Leadbelly found a larger audience for his music.**

   In 1934, he was discovered by John and Alan Lomax, who helped him find a larger audience for his music.

   Soon he was playing in colleges, clubs, and music halls.

   Everywhere

English Language Arts

Strategy Review

Strategy   Use an outline to plan your writing.

When you have a writing assignment and not much time to plan, a scratch outline can help you quickly pull together ideas. These outlines get their name from the way they're written—very quickly and informally, maybe even scratched on a sheet of paper. A quick look at this outline shows that the writer has not gathered all the information needed for the opinion essay.

Scratch Outline for an Argument

STEP 1: Make a claim.
My claim: *All students should participate in a fine arts class.*

STEP 2: Consider the evidence.

My list of evidence for my claim:	My list of evidence against my claim:
1. *Fine arts classes take up schedule time.* 2. *Fine arts classes build friendships and camaraderie.* 3. *Fine arts students may earn college scholarships.*	1. *Music takes lots of time and effort* 2. *Musical instruments and art are expensive.* 3. *What if you are not good at fine arts?*

Position: Investing time and funds in fine arts participation for students is a good idea because . . .

1. **Based on the outline, what does the writer need to do before drafting her argument?**

   She needs to do a little more research and then structure her argument in CER.

English Language Arts

Strategy Review

> "Bigger is better" is an idea that many people agree with when it comes to homes. It is nice to have a large living space so that children can have their own rooms and adults can add an office or guest room. _____, some people prefer to live in so-called tiny houses. These houses range in size from just a few hundred square feet to about a thousand square feet. Some tiny houses are built on trailers so that they can be moved from place to place. People who move into a tiny house have to "downsize," or give away many of their possessions. Many are willing to do this _____ a tiny house gives them the freedom to live in beautiful places near mountains or beaches, where they could not afford to live otherwise.

When you write an argument, you may need to present a commonly held idea and then propose a new idea in its place. Transitions that signal contrast, such as *but* and *on the other hand*, help you guide readers from the commonly held idea to your new idea. You can then use cause and effect transitions, such as *because* or *as a result* to explain why your new idea is worth hearing.

Strategy   Use transitions to show how ideas are related in an argument.

1. **Write a transition in the first blank to help readers move from the commonly held idea to the writer's new idea. Write a transition in the second blank to show why the new idea is worth hearing.**

_____ In fact _____
_____ because, _____

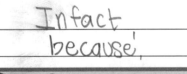 **Strategy**

Revise to make sure your writing is clear and makes sense. Then, edit to fix errors.

Successful authors often state that writing is revising. What do they mean by this? They mean that a writer's first draft, or even second or third draft, is often not ready to be published. Writing drafts helps writers explore and develop their ideas. For example, a writer may have an idea for a character who is stealthy, small, and whiskered. By revising drafts, the writer will get to know the character and, then, be able to describe the character to readers more fully:

> The other mice called him "Mouse-master" for good reason. Though he was small, he was the quickest of all of the mice, and he knew passages through the house's walls that had never been mapped.

2. **Write another revision tip that a writer could use to describe "Mouse-master." Then, write a sentence about Mouse-master using that tip.**

The writer could have described the Mouse-master in detail. The Mouse-master was as tiny as a cell and quiter than a whisper.

Strategies for Mathematics Tests

Use rules, properties, or formulas to solve problems.

You can use rules, properties, and formulas to solve a variety of problems. For example, if you know the formula for the area of a rectangle, you can use a given length and width of the rectangle to quickly find its area. If you understand the commutative and distributive properties, you can rearrange an equation to solve it. If you understand the rules of the order of operations, you can correctly evaluate a mathematical expression.

Use drawings, graphs, or number lines to understand and solve a problem.

Many problems on a test can be modeled with a quick sketch, graph, or number line. These drawings can help you visualize the problem, figure out what you are being asked to find, or solve word problems.

Read word problems carefully to identify the given information and what you are being asked to find.

Whenever you encounter a word problem, you should first ask *What is the given information?* Then, you should ask *What question am I being asked to answer?* or *What am I being asked to find?* Don't start your calculations until you know the answers to these questions!

Look for key words in word problems that help you know which operation to use.

Key words in problems are signals that you should use certain operations. For example, the words *how much less* indicate subtraction. The words *total* and *altogether* often indicate addition. If you are asked to split something into equal portions, use division.

Organize and display data in order to interpret it.

Interpreting data means finding meaning in it. One way to find meaning in data is to organize it in a visual way. For example, dot plots are great for understanding data from a survey or poll. Line graphs show how two sets of data are related.

Apply prior knowledge and basic operations to solve problems.

Using what you already know about numbers and about the basic operations addition, subtraction, multiplication, and division, you can solve problems involving decimals, fractions, geometry, and converting units of measurement. For example, you can use your understanding of division, multiplication, and place value to find area and to convert meters to centimeters.

Write and solve equations to solve real-world problems.

Translating everyday language into equations that use numbers, variables, and operations signs is an essential strategy. You will need to combine your understanding of several strategies to write and solve these equations, including understanding basic operations; applying rules, properties, and formulas; and looking for clues in the words to find needed information.

Understand Ratios
Ratios and Proportional Relationships

DIRECTIONS: Choose or write the correct answer.

> ### Strategy
> Describe real-world situations using ratios.

1. What would be the ratio of wings to beaks in the bird house at the zoo?

   (A) 2:1

   (B) 1:2

   (C) It depends on how many birds there are.

   (D) It depends on what types of birds are in the house.

   Write how you know.

   _____

   _____

2. Write a situation for which the ratio 4:3 would be used.

   _____

   _____

3. In the election for class president, Cole received 186 votes and Lauren received 62 votes. Write a ratio to show the results of the election.

   _____

   Explain your ratio in words.

   _____

   _____

4. Which two statements match the ratio 10:1?

   (A) For every vote Candidate B received, Candidate A received 10.

   (B) Suzanne ran 10 miles on Saturday and 1 mile on Sunday.

   (C) To make a bubble solution, use 10 parts water and 1 part soap.

   (D) I have $10 in one of my bank accounts.

5. The concession sells hamburgers and hot dogs. On Friday night, the stand sold 127 hot dogs. It sold 254 hamburgers. What is the ratio of hot dogs sold to hamburgers sold? What is the ratio of hot dogs sold to the total number of hamburgers and hot dogs sold?

   _____

   Explain your ratios in words.

   _____

   _____

   _____

   _____

   _____

Understand Unit Rates
Ratios and Proportional Relationships

DIRECTIONS: Choose or write the correct answer.

Strategy Express unit rates as ratios and as fractions to show relationships between numbers.

Test Tip Remember, a unit rate is a ratio and can be expressed as a fraction. A unit rate expressed as a fraction must always have a 1 in the denominator. For example, 35 miles per hour is written as $\frac{35}{1}$.

1. **A recipe calls for 3 cups of flour for every cup of sugar. What is the ratio of flour to sugar written as a unit rate?**

   (A) 3:4

   (B) $\frac{3}{4}$:1

   (C) 4:1

   (D) 3:$\frac{1}{4}$

2. **The Lady Mustangs scored 102 points in their game against the Lincoln Knights. Write the average number of points scored per quarter as a unit rate.**

   _____

3. **The Davis family paid $75 for 15 hamburgers. This is a rate of $5 per burger. Explain how this rate was found.**

   _____

   _____

   _____

4. **Alice traveled 330 miles in 6 hours. What was her speed, expressed as a unit rate?**

   (A) 330 miles per 6 hours

   (B) 165 miles per 3 hours

   (C) 110 miles per 2 hours

   (D) 55 miles per hour

Write how you found your answer.

_____

_____

5. **A 3-pound bag of carrots costs $3.25. A 5-pound bag of carrots costs $4.75. Which is the better deal?**

   _____

Write how you know.

_____

_____

_____

_____

_____

_____

Use Rates and Ratios
Ratios and Proportional Relationships

DIRECTIONS: Choose or write the correct answer.

Strategy   Apply unit rates and ratios to real-life situations.

1. **Find the missing values in the ratio table.**

Dogs	1	2	3	4
Cats	3	6	9	12

   Write the equivalent ratios from the table.

   $1:3 :: 2:6 :: 3:9 :: 4:12$

2. **Your parents are having a garage sale, and you want to make some money too. You decide to sell lemonade. To make a gallon of lemonade, you need $1\frac{1}{2}$ cups of lemonade mix to 1 gallon of water. You want to make a 5-gallon batch of lemonade. Complete the ratio table to find out how much lemonade mix you will need.**

Lemonade (gallons)	1	2	3	4	5
Lemonade mix (cups)	1.5	3	4.5	6	7.5

   How many cups of lemonade mix will you need?

   7.5 cups

Test Tip

A tape diagram is a way to visualize ratios.

3. **The tape diagram below shows the ratio of Brody's violin practice hours to Kendall's cello practice hours.**

   Brody's violin practice

   Kendall's cello practice

Write a ratio to compare the number of hours Brody practices to the number of hours Kendall practices.

5 : 3

4. **Use the double number line to find the cost of 3 sweaters.**

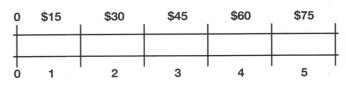

Write a unit rate to show the cost per sweater.

I sweater is to $15.

5. **Write a scenario that uses the ratio 3:8.**

You have 3 sweaters for $8. Find the unit rate.

Use Rates and Ratios
Ratios and Proportional Relationships

DIRECTIONS: Choose or write the correct answer.

Strategy Use ratios and rates to express comparisons and make decisions.

6. A cheetah can run up to 60 miles per hour. Which equation shows how fast a cheetah could run in 45 minutes?

Ⓐ $60 \times 45 = 2,700$

Ⓑ $60 \div 12 = 1.33$

Ⓒ $\frac{3}{4} \times 60 = 45$

Ⓓ $\frac{60}{45} \times 60 = 80$

7. Caroline looked at a website to buy dog food. The website she looked at sells three different brands. Use the table to decide which brand is the best value.

Brand	Puppy Protein	Delicious Dog Food	YUM Dog Food
Size	14 pounds	17 pounds	15 pounds
Price	$17.50	$19.55	$19.50

The best value is
Delicious Dog Food.

Explain how you know your answer is correct.

First, I found the
unit rate by dividing
size and price. Then, I
compared the rates.

8. U.S. nuclear submarines can travel 25 nautical miles per hour under water. Complete the table to show how far a submarine can travel in 5, 10, and 15 hours.

Nautical Miles	25	125	250	375
Hour	1	5	10	15

9. A box of cereal has a calorie-to-serving ratio of 114:1. If a serving is one cup, how many calories are there in $3\frac{1}{2}$ cups of the cereal?

Ⓐ 32.57

Ⓑ 117.5

Ⓒ 399

Ⓓ 342

10. Write a scenario that uses the ratio 4:7.

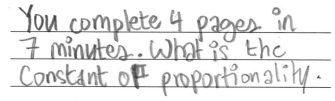

You complete 4 pages in
7 minutes. What is the
Constant of proportionality.

Use Percents
Ratios and Proportional Relationships

DIRECTIONS: Choose or write the correct answer.

Strategy Use multiplication, division, and proportions to find answers to percent problems.

1. **What is 62% of 72?**
   - (A) 44.64
   - (B) 0.009
   - (C) 4,464
   - (D) 10

2. **What is 73% of 87?**
   - (A) 20
   - (B) 6,351
   - (C) 0.839
   - (D) 63.51

3. **Write each fraction as a percent.**

   $\frac{3}{5}$ _____

   $\frac{6}{9}$ _____

   $\frac{5}{8}$ _____

   $\frac{6}{7}$ _____

4. **Write each fraction as a percent.**

   $\frac{4}{5}$ _____

   $\frac{3}{8}$ _____

   $\frac{5}{3}$ _____

   $\frac{7}{9}$ _____

Strategy

The proportion $\frac{a}{b} = \frac{p}{100}$ can help you find the answer to percent problems.

5. **Pizzazz Pizza Parlor gave the sixth-grade class a 25% discount on pizzas they purchased for a party. Each pizza originally cost $12.00. How much did the sixth graders pay per pizza?**
   - (A) $3.00
   - (B) $9.00
   - (C) $8.00
   - (D) $6.00

6. **Twenty-five percent of the workers are on third shift. There are 33 workers on third shift. How many workers are there total? Show your work.**

7. **Forty percent of the members of the drama club are boys. There are 55 members of drama club. How many are girls? Show your work.**

Name _____

Math

Convert Measurement Units
Ratios and Proportional Relationships

DIRECTIONS: Choose or write the correct answer.

Strategy   Convert from one unit to another using proportions.

Test Tip   Use the equivalency table to help you create your proportions.

1 gallon = 4 quarts	1 foot = 12 inches
2 pints = 1 quart	1 centimeter = 10 millimeters
2 cups = 1 pint	1 kilogram = 1,000 grams
8 fluid ounces = 1 cup	1 gram = 1,000 milligrams
1 yard = 3 feet	

1. A recipe calls for 6 quarts of water. How many gallons is that?

   (A) 1 gallon

   (B) $1\frac{1}{2}$ gallons

   (C) 2 gallons

   (D) $2\frac{1}{2}$ gallons

2. Kenny's book is 30 millimeters thick. How many centimeters thick is the book?

   _____ 3 cm _____

3. A football field is 100 yards long. Use proportions to find out how many inches long a football field is.

   1y = 36 in

   100 × 36

   = 3600 in

4. Sixteen cups is equivalent to all of the following except _____?

   (A) 8 pints

   (B) 1 gallon

   (C) 4 quarts

   (D) 100 fluid ounces

5. A gallon of milk costs $3.25. How much does it cost per 1-cup serving? Show your work.

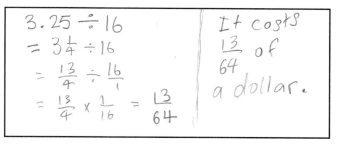

   $3.25 \div 16$
   $= 3\frac{1}{4} \div 16$
   $= \frac{13}{4} \div \frac{16}{1}$
   $= \frac{13}{4} \times \frac{1}{16} = \frac{13}{64}$

   It costs $\frac{13}{64}$ of a dollar.

Divide Fractions
The Number System

DIRECTIONS: Choose or write the correct answer.

> **Strategy**   Use multiplication to divide fractions.

> **Test Tip**   Remember to multiply by the reciprocal when dividing fractions.

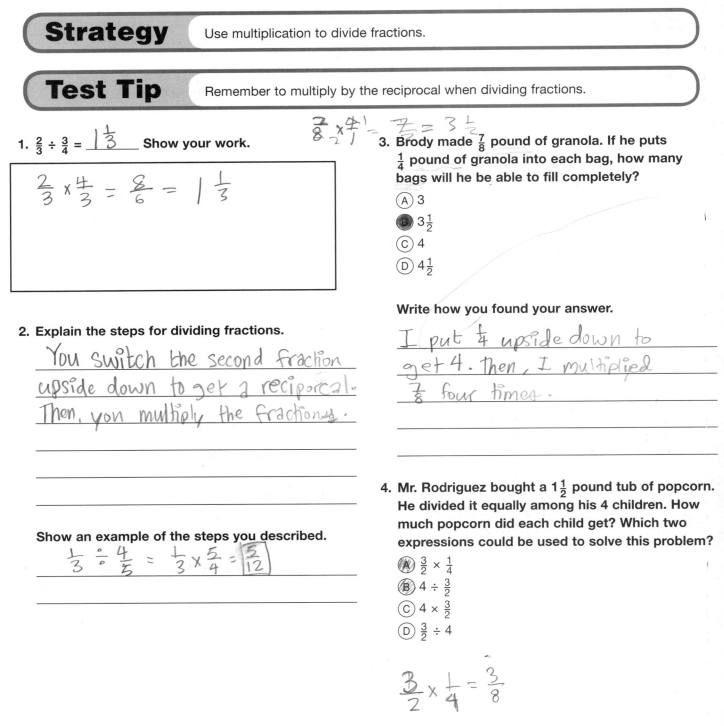

1. $\frac{2}{3} \div \frac{3}{4} =$ $1\frac{1}{3}$ **Show your work.**

$$\frac{2}{3} \times \frac{4}{3} = \frac{8}{6} = 1\frac{1}{3}$$

2. **Explain the steps for dividing fractions.**

You switch the second fraction upside down to get a reciporcal. Then, you multiply the fractions.

Show an example of the steps you described.

$$\frac{1}{3} \div \frac{4}{5} = \frac{1}{3} \times \frac{5}{4} = \frac{5}{12}$$

$$\frac{7}{8} \times \frac{4}{1} = \frac{7}{2} = 3\frac{1}{2}$$

3. Brody made $\frac{7}{8}$ pound of granola. If he puts $\frac{1}{4}$ pound of granola into each bag, how many bags will he be able to fill completely?

Ⓐ 3
Ⓑ $3\frac{1}{2}$
Ⓒ 4
Ⓓ $4\frac{1}{2}$

Write how you found your answer.

I put $\frac{1}{4}$ upside down to get 4. then, I multiplied $\frac{7}{8}$ four times.

4. Mr. Rodriguez bought a $1\frac{1}{2}$ pound tub of popcorn. He divided it equally among his 4 children. How much popcorn did each child get? Which two expressions could be used to solve this problem?

Ⓐ $\frac{3}{2} \times \frac{1}{4}$
Ⓑ $4 \div \frac{3}{2}$
Ⓒ $4 \times \frac{3}{2}$
Ⓓ $\frac{3}{2} \div 4$

$$\frac{3}{2} \times \frac{1}{4} = \frac{3}{8}$$

Divide Fractions
The Number System

DIRECTIONS: Choose or write the correct answer.

Strategy Divide fractions to solve real-world problems.

5. How many $\frac{1}{3}$ cup servings are in $\frac{3}{4}$ cup of yogurt?

(A) $2\frac{1}{4}$

(B) $\frac{1}{12}$

(C) $\frac{1}{2}$

(D) $\frac{4}{7}$

6. What is the area of a canyon with a length of $\frac{1}{2}$ mile and a width of 2.25 miles? Show your work.

$2.25 = 2\frac{1}{4}$

$2\frac{1}{4} \times \frac{1}{2}$

$= \frac{9}{4} \times \frac{1}{2}$

$= \frac{9}{8}$

$= 1\frac{1}{8}$

$1\frac{1}{8}$ miles

7. How long is a park with a width of $\frac{3}{4}$ mile and an area of 1.5 square miles? Show your work.

$1.5 = 1\frac{1}{2}$

$1\frac{1}{2} \mid \frac{3}{4}$

$= \frac{3}{2} \times \frac{4}{3}$

$= 2$

2 miles

8. Brooke ran for $\frac{3}{4}$ hour. She ran a total of $2\frac{1}{3}$ miles. What was her speed in miles per hour? Show your work.

$2\frac{1}{3} \mid \frac{3}{4}$

$= \frac{7}{3} \times \frac{4}{3}$

$= \frac{28}{9}$

$= 3\frac{1}{9}$

9. How much chocolate candy will each child get if 3 children share a $\frac{1}{4}$ pound bag of chocolate candies?

_____ $\frac{1}{12}$ lb chocolate

$\frac{1}{4} \div 3$

$= \frac{1}{4} \times \frac{1}{3}$

$= \frac{1}{12}$

Draw a visual fraction model to illustrate your answer.

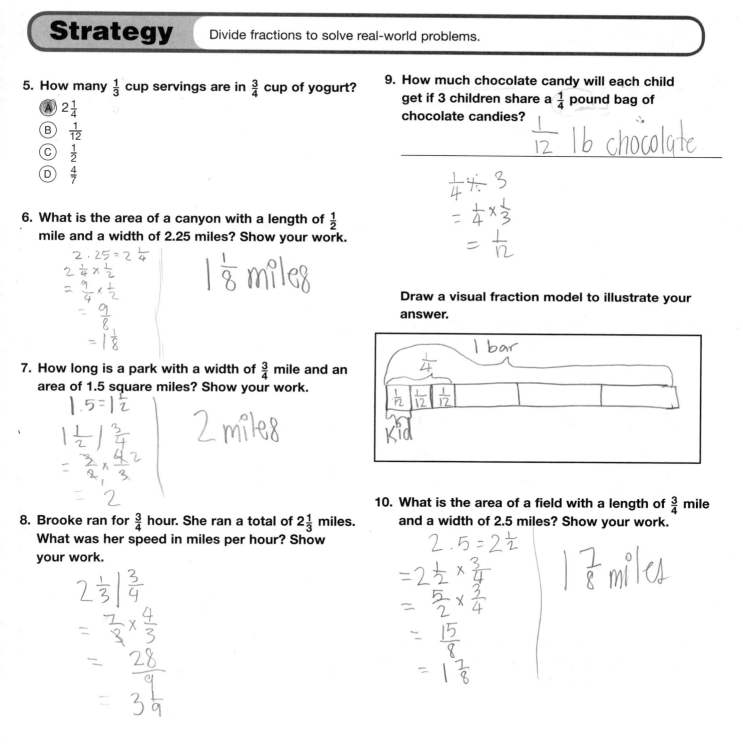

10. What is the area of a field with a length of $\frac{3}{4}$ mile and a width of 2.5 miles? Show your work.

$2.5 = 2\frac{1}{2}$

$= 2\frac{1}{2} \times \frac{3}{4}$

$= \frac{5}{2} \times \frac{3}{4}$

$= \frac{15}{8}$

$= 1\frac{7}{8}$

$1\frac{7}{8}$ miles

Divide Multi-Digit Numbers
The Number System

DIRECTIONS: Choose or write the correct answer.

Strategy Follow the steps of long division to complete long division with multi-digit numbers.

Test Tip Remember to follow the steps of standard division: Divide, Multiply, Subtract, Bring Down, Repeat.

1. 4,281 ÷ 3 = _____

Write how you know.

_____

_____

2. **A student completed the division problem below. Explain the student's error and give the correct quotient.**

```
        21
32 ) 6848
    - 64
      44
    - 32
      28
```

The quotient is 21 r28.

_____

_____

_____

_____

3. **A pet store has 450 goldfish. They want to divide the fish equally into 18 tanks. How many goldfish should they put in each tank?**

(A) 8,100

(B) 432

(C) 25

(D) 468

4. **The Mason family is planning a summer road trip. They want to travel for 14 days, for a total distance of 2,317 miles. How many miles should they travel each day?**

(A) 166

(B) 165

(C) 165 r7

(D) 165.5

5. **Ms. Raphael is pouring lemonade into cups for a party. She begins with 4,000 mL. She pours 280 mL into each cup. How many cups can she fill? Explain how you found your answer.**

_____

_____

_____

_____

_____

Compute with Decimals
The Number System

DIRECTIONS: Choose or write the correct answer.

Strategy Look for key words in word problems that help you determine which operation to use.

1. The average annual temperature in Death Valley, California is 77.2°F. The average annual temperature in Anchorage, Alaska is 37°F. On average, how much warmer is it in Death Valley than in Anchorage?

   _____

   Write why you chose the operation you did.

   _____

   _____

   _____

   _____

2. According to the nutritional information on the box, a serving of crackers has 3.5 grams of fat. If there are 9 crackers in a serving, how many grams of fat would be in each cracker?

   (A) about 12.5 grams

   (B) about 6.5 grams

   (C) about 0.39 grams

   (D) about 31.5 grams

   Write why you chose the operation you did.

   _____

   _____

   _____

   _____

   _____

3. A flight attendant flew 4 flights in 3 days. On Monday, she flew 1,275.3 miles. On Tuesday, she flew 514.5 miles. On Wednesday, she flew two flights. One flight was 2,050.15 miles, and the other was 362.175 miles. How many miles did she accumulate during the 3 days?

4. Sean's car gets 36.9 miles per gallon. How many gallons of gas would Sean need to travel 250 miles?

   (A) 9,225

   (B) 6.8

   (C) 0.148

   (D) 286.9

   If gas costs $3.29 per gallon, how much will it cost Sean to make this trip? Show your work.

Compute with Decimals
The Number System

DIRECTIONS: Choose or write the correct answer.

> **Strategy** Use basic operations to solve real-world problems involving money.

5. Else, Sienna, and Alexa bought a gift for their mother. The total price for the gift was $112.32. How much did each sister pay if they split the total evenly? Show your work.

Write how you know.

_____

_____

_____

_____

_____

6. Explain the error and give the correct product.

```
      27.4
   ×  1.36
   ───────
      1644
      8220
  +  27400
   ───────
    372.64
```

_____

_____

_____

_____

8. Reese went back-to-school shopping. She bought 3 sweaters at $19.99 each, 4 pairs of jeans at 2 for $50.50, and a pair of shoes for $75.25. Her mother agreed to pay for half the clothing bill. How much did Reese pay? Show your work.

7. Jeremiah received a $50 gift card for a video game store. He purchased Krazy Karts for $29.99, Sumo Superstar for $27.50, and a new controller for $15.99. The tax came to $4.41. After using the gift card, how much did Jeremiah have to pay?

Ⓐ $77.89

Ⓑ $17.89

Ⓒ $127.89

Ⓓ $27.89

9. A family drove 358.15 miles on Friday. On, Saturday, they drove 426.3 miles. On Sunday, they drove 504.5 miles. How many miles did they drive in all?

Find GCF and LCM
The Number System

DIRECTIONS: Choose or write the correct answer.

Strategy — Use different strategies, such as making a list, factor tree, or factor rainbow, to answer the questions.

Test Tip — Don't be afraid to try more than one strategy to find one that works.

1. **What is the least common multiple of 8 and 12?**
   (A) 12
   (B) 16
   (C) 24
   (D) 30

   Write how you know.

   _____

   _____

   _____

   _____

   _____

   _____

2. **For reasons known only to the hot dog industry, hot dogs come in packages of 10, and hot dog buns come in packages of 8. How many packages of each would you have to buy to have the same number of hot dogs and buns? Choose two.**
   (A) 4 packages of hot dogs
   (B) 5 packages of hot dogs
   (C) 4 packages of buns
   (D) 5 packages of buns

3. **Find the greatest common factor of 12 and 16. Show your work.**

4. **Asher has 48 baseball cards and 64 football cards. He wants to put them into an album so that each page has only baseball or football cards on it. What is the greatest number of cards he can put on a page so that all the pages have the same number of cards?**
   (A) 2
   (B) 4
   (C) 16
   (D) 32

   How many pages will Asher need in his album?

   _____

Use the Distributive Property
The Number System

DIRECTIONS: Choose or write the correct answer.

Strategy Use the Distributive Property to solve problems.

Test Tip The Distributive Property states that a common factor can be multiplied through an addition or subtraction problem. For example: $3(8 + 4) = (3 \times 8) + (3 \times 4)$.

1. **Which expressions are equivalent?**
   - (A) 36 + 8
   - (B) 4 (9 + 2)
   - (C) 3 (12 + 8)
   - (D) 2 (18 + 4)

2. **A student wrote the following on his math homework assignment:**

   6 (12 − 8) = 64

   Explain the error in the equation and give the correct answer.

   $6\left(4\right)$
   $= 24$

3. **A desk normally costs $129. It is on sale for $99. Which expression would tell you how much you would save if you bought 2 desks on sale?**
   - (A) 2 ($129 + $99) =
   - (B) ($129 − $99) ÷ 2 =
   - (C) 2 ($129 − $99) =
   - (D) ($129 + $99) ÷ 2 =

   How much would you save?

   $ 60

4. **Evaluate the expressions. Show each step of the Distributive Property.**
   - (A) 5 (10 − 7) = _50 − 35_ = _15_
   - (B) 3 (12 + 25) = _36 + 75_ = _111_
   - (C) 7 (8 − 7) = _56 − 49_ = _7_
   - (D) 4 (100 + 5) = _400 + 20_ = _420_

5. **Skye uses 16 red beads and 8 gold beads to make one necklace. Write an expression to show how many beads she will need if she makes 15 necklaces.**

   $15\left(16 + 8\right)$

   If each bead costs $0.32, how much will she need to spend to make the 15 necklaces?

   $ 115.20

Use Positive and Negative Numbers
The Number System

DIRECTIONS: Choose or write the correct answer.

Strategy Apply an understanding of the number line to help explain real-world situations.

1. The coldest recorded temperature in Antarctica was −135.8°F. This temperature is _____.
Choose two.

   Ⓐ 135.8° below zero
   Ⓑ 135.8° above zero
   Ⓒ colder than freezing (32°F)
   Ⓓ warmer than freezing (32°F)

   Write how you know.

   It is under frezzing.
   Zero.

2. Write a number that represents this phrase:
The peak of Mt. Kilimanjaro is 19,341 feet above sea level.

   _+19,341_

   In this situation, what does zero represent?

   _0_

3. Write a number that represents this phrase:
The lowest land area in Africa is 502 feet below sea level.

   _−502_

   In this situation, what does zero represent?

   _0_

4. The Royal Gorge in Colorado is 1,200 feet deep at its deepest.

   Which number represents the depth of the Royal Gorge?

   _−1200_

   What does zero represent?

   _0_

5. Write a scenario that could represent the number −15.

   You are 15 foot underground.

Name _____ Date _____

Math

Understand Rational Numbers
The Number System

DIRECTIONS: Choose or write the correct answer.

> **Strategy**   Use drawings, graphs, or number lines to understand and solve a problem.

1. Place the following points on the number line.

    J –4   **K** 6.5   **L** –0.5   **M** 2

(number line from -10 to 10 with points J, L, M, K marked)
-10 -8 -6 -4 -2 0 2 4 6 8 10

2. Label this portion of the number line to show the range of –15 to –20. Place a point at –16.5.

(number line labeled) −20 −19 −18 −17 −16 −15, point marked −16.5

3. Which number line correctly shows the number 21.5?

(A) -25 -24 -23 -22 -21 -20 *(point between -21 and -20)*

(B) 20 21 22 23 24 25 *(point between 20 and 21)*

(C) -25 -24 -23 -22 -21 -20 *(point between -21 and -20)*

(D) 20 21 22 23 24 25 *(point between 21 and 22)*

4. Label this portion of the number line to show the range of 125 to 130. Place a point at 126.

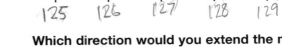
125 126 127 128 129 130

Which direction would you extend the number line to plot a point at 107?

To the left

5. Which number line correctly shows the number –24.5?

(A) -25 -24 -23 -22 -21 -20 *(point between -24 and -23... at -24)*

(B) 20 21 22 23 24 25 *(point between 24 and 25)*

(C) -25 -24 -23 -22 -21 -20 *(point between -25 and -24)*

(D) 20 21 22 23 24 25 *(point between 22 and 23)*

Understand Rational Numbers
The Number System

DIRECTIONS: Choose or write the correct answer.

Strategy | Use coordinate pairs to graph points and to describe locations on a coordinate plane.

Test Tip | Points on a graph are labeled using coordinate pairs. The first value in the pair represents the horizontal distance from zero. A positive number means to move right. A negative number means to move left. The second value in the pair represents the vertical distance from zero. A positive number means to move up. A negative number means to move down.

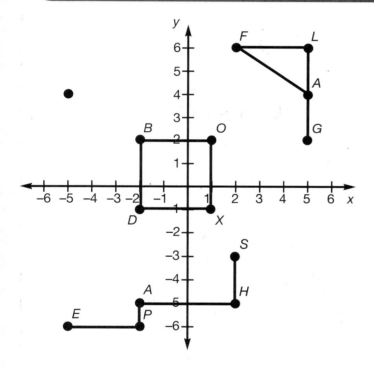

BOXD

B = (-2 , 2)
O = (1 , 2)
X = (1 , -1)
D = (-2 , -1)

SHAPE

S = (2 , -3)
H = (2 , -5)
A = (-2 , -5)
P = (-2 , -6)
E = (-5 , -6)

6. Write the ordered pairs for each figure plotted.

FLAG

F = (2 , 6)
L = (5 , 6)
A = (5 , 4)
G = (5 , 2)

7. Plot the following points on the coordinate plane.

W (−6, −4)
X (0, 6)
Y (−5, 0)
Z (3, −2)

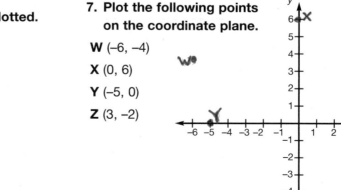

Understand Rational Numbers
The Number System

DIRECTIONS: Choose or write the correct answer.

> **Strategy**   Visualize the location of positive and negative numbers on a number line to answer questions about order, opposites, and absolute value.

> **Test Tip**   Read all parts of the question first.

1. **Order the numbers from least to greatest.**

   –4, 5, –8, 1, 6, –2

   _–8, –4, –2, 1, 5, 6_

   6.5, 6.25, –3.7, –3.12, 6

   _–3.7, –3.12, 6, 6.25, 6.5_

   –0.5, 0, –0.25, –0.14, 0.5, 0.34

   _–.5, –.25, –.14, .34, .5_

   2, 2.2, –1.5, –1.8, 2.12

   _–1.8, –1.5, 2, 2.2, 2.12_

2. **Complete the table. For each number, write its opposite and its absolute value.**

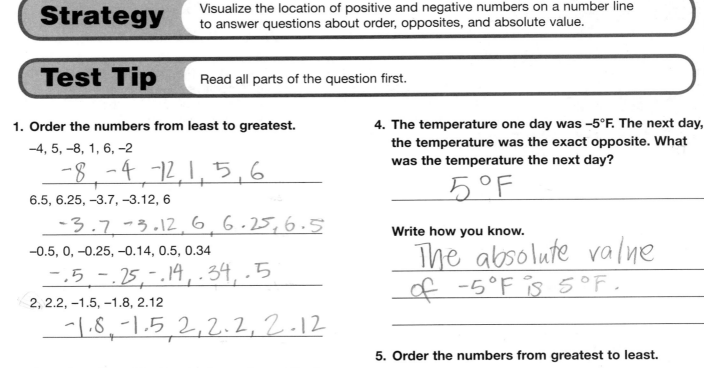

Number	Opposite	Absolute Value
1.7	–1.7	1.7
0	0	0
-3.5	3.5	3.5
-10	10	10
0.61	–.61	0.61

3. **Which list shows the numbers in order from least to greatest?**

   Ⓐ 0, –5, –10, –11.5, –15

   Ⓑ 5, –5, 6, –6, 18, –18

   Ⓒ –25, –17, –8, 0, 5

   Ⓓ –14, –12, –10, 14, 12, 10

4. **The temperature one day was –5°F. The next day, the temperature was the exact opposite. What was the temperature the next day?**

   _5 °F_

   Write how you know.

   The absolute value
   _of –5°F is 5°F._

5. **Order the numbers from greatest to least.**

   –5, 13, |–5|, |–12|, –15, 15, |–17|, 0

   _17, 15, 13, 12, 0, –5, –15_

Understand Rational Numbers
The Number System

DIRECTIONS: Choose or write the correct answer.

Strategy   Use visuals such as number lines or charts to help you understand a problem.

6. Write a situation for this inequality: –12°F < –7°F

_____

_____

7. The table shows the temperatures in Iowa for one week in December.

Monday	–5°F
Tuesday	–3°F
Wednesday	2°F
Thursday	–4°F
Friday	–4°F

Which day was the coldest?

_____

Write an inequality that compares the temperatures on Wednesday and Friday.

_____

8. On a coordinate grid, a point is plotted at (–7, 5). How far from zero is the point on the y-axis?

Ⓐ –7 units

Ⓑ –5 units

Ⓒ 5 units

Ⓓ 7 units

Use absolute value notation to explain the correct answer.

_____

9. Clara and Paige both overdrew their checking accounts. Clara has a balance of –$17.24. Paige has a balance of –$25.01. Who needs to deposit more money to reach a balance of $0?

_____

Write an inequality that compares the girls' balances.

_____

10. Nathaniel loves to use coupons. He can buy hundreds of dollars of groceries for only a few dollars. On one shopping trip, Nathaniel looked at his receipt and saw a total of –$1.75. What does this mean for Nathaniel?

_____

_____

11. If a submarine dives to –300 feet, what is its absolute distance from the surface of the water?

_____

Where would the opposite of the sub's position be?

_____

_____

Name _____   Date _____

Math

Use a Coordinate Plane
The Number System

DIRECTIONS: Rudi made a map of her classroom in the form of a coordinate plane. Each number along the *x-* and *y-axes* represents one foot. Use Rudi's map to answer the questions.

Strategy   Use a coordinate plane to understand and solve a problem.

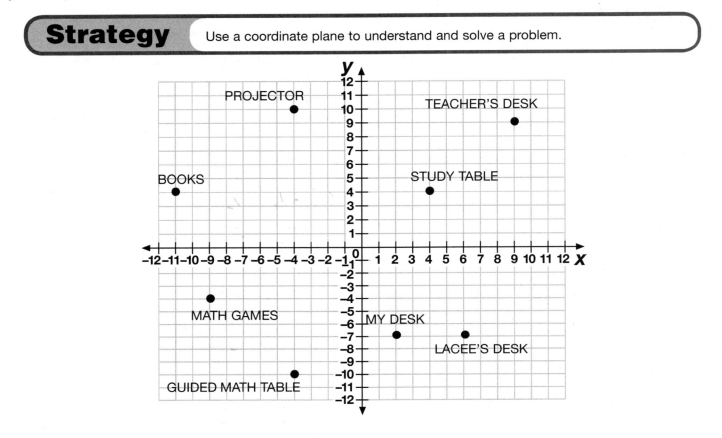

1. **Describe how to get to the book area from the study table.**

   From table, move 15 units the left.

2. **Which item is exactly opposite the projector?**
   - (A) teacher's desk
   - (B) books
   - (C) guided math table
   - (D) my desk

3. **How far from Lacee's desk is Rudi's desk?**

   4 units

   Write how you know.

   From Lacee's desk to Rudi's desk, it is 4 units left.

Name _____ Date _10-7-19_

Math

Use a Coordinate Plane
The Number System

DIRECTIONS: Follow the steps below to make a map of Rudi's town. Each number on the axes represents 1 mile.

Strategy | Create or refer to visuals as often as needed to understand and solve a problem.

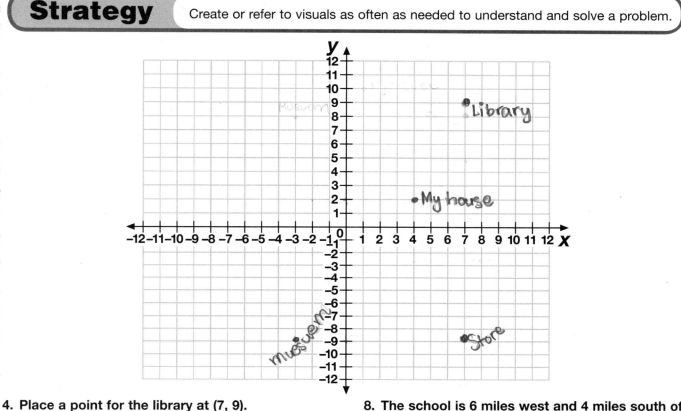

4. Place a point for the library at (7, 9).

5. Going south, place a point opposite the library. Label it store.

   What is the ordered pair for the store?

   (7, -9)

6. Move 10 miles west from the store. Place a point labeled museum at this point.

7. Go 2 miles north and 4 miles east from the center of town (origin). Place a point labeled my house.

   What is the ordered pair for Rudi's house?

   (4, 2)

8. The school is 6 miles west and 4 miles south of Rudi's house. What is the ordered pair for the school?

   (A) (6, 2)
   (B) (2, 6)
   (C) (0, 0)
   (D) (–2, –2)

9. Lacee's house is 7 miles east, opposite the school. What is the ordered pair for Lacee's house?

   (5, -2)

Evaluate Exponents
Expressions and Equations

DIRECTIONS: Choose or write the correct answer.

Strategy | Evaluate expressions with exponents using multiplication.

Test Tip | Remember that an exponent tells how many times to multiply the base by itself. For example, 7^3 means $7 \times 7 \times 7$, not 7×3.

1. Complete the table.

$2 \times 2 \times 2 \times 2 \times 2$	2^5
	3^4
8×8	
$6 \times 6 \times 6$	
	1^7

2. What is the value of 8^4?
   - (A) 32
   - (B) 12
   - (C) 4,096
   - (D) 16

Write how you used multiplication to find the answer.

_____

_____

_____

_____

3. A square has a side length of 5 feet. What exponent expression can you write to find the area?

_____

What if the square were one side of cube? What exponent expression could you use to find the volume of the cube?

_____

4. A clown is holding 6 balloons. Inside each balloon are 6 coins. On each coin are 6 dots. How many dots are there?
   - (A) 18
   - (B) 6
   - (C) 216
   - (D) 36

Write how you found your answer.

_____

_____

_____

_____

_____

5. Write a story like the one above for the expression 44.

_____

_____

_____

_____

_____

_____

Name _____ Date _____

Math

Understand Expressions
Expressions and Equations

DIRECTIONS: Choose or write the correct answer.

Strategy | Write expressions to represent real-world situations, then evaluate the expressions to find unknown values.

1. Write an expression to represent *y* less than 5.

_____ $y < 5$ _____

2. Which expressions match the words *the sum of x and 7*? Choose two.

Ⓐ $x - 7$

Ⓑ $7x$

● $x + 7$

Ⓓ $7 + x$

3. In the equation $3x + 7 = 22$, name the...

terms $3x, 7, 22$

sum 15

coefficient 3

variable x

Test Tip

Remember that a variable represents an unknown number.
---

4. Evaluate the expressions when $a = 5$, $b = 3$, and $c = 7$

$4a + b$ 23

$a(b + 4)$ 35

$ac - 2b$ 29

$a^2 - b^2$ 16

5. Use the formulas $V = s^3$ and $A = 6s^2$ to find the volume and surface area of a cube with sides of length $s = \frac{1}{2}$. Show your work.

$V = \boxed{\dfrac{1}{8}^3}$ $\dfrac{1}{2} \cdot \dfrac{1}{2} \cdot \dfrac{1}{2} = \dfrac{1}{8}$

$A = \boxed{1\frac{1}{2}}$

6. Evaluate $2a - 3b + 4c$, when $a = 4$, $b = 3$, and $c = 2$.

Ⓐ 25

Ⓑ 38

● 7

Ⓓ 12

7. Evaluate $3a + 4b + 6c$, when $a = 5$, $b = 4$, and $c = 3$.

Ⓐ 13

● 49

Ⓒ 19

Ⓓ 62

Understanding Expressions
Expressions and Equations

Test Tip   Find the variable in an expression or equation. Common variables to use are *x*, *n*, and *y*. Any letter can be used as a variable in an expression or equation.

8. Kate is twice as old as Nathaniel. Write an expression to show this relationship. Let Nathaniel's age = *n*.

_____

9. Micah sold 3 times as many pizzas as Sadie and Jason sold altogether. Which expression shows this relationship?

   Ⓐ $3 + s + j$

   Ⓑ $(s + j) - 3$

   Ⓒ $3(s + j)$

   Ⓓ $3sj$

10. Three children evenly shared $\frac{1}{2}$ bag of cookies. Which expressions show this relationship?

   Ⓐ $\frac{1}{2}c \div 3$

   Ⓑ $\frac{1}{2}c \times \frac{1}{3}$

   Ⓒ $3(\frac{1}{2}c)$

   Ⓓ $\dfrac{\frac{1}{2}c}{3}$

11. Write a situation to match the expression $3k - 7$.

_____

_____

_____

Evaluate the expression for *k* = 3.

_____

12. In one town, police calculate speeding tickets with this formula: $50 + 10m$. The first 10 miles per hour over the speed limit is a flat $50 fine. For each additional mile per hour over the speed limit, there is an additional $10 charged. What would the speeding ticket be for a person traveling 60 miles per hour in a 35–mile-per-hour zone?

What would the speeding ticket be for a person traveling 90 miles per hour in a 55–mile-per-hour zone?

What would the speed ticket be for a person traveling 80 miles per hour in a 65-mile-per-hour-zone?

Name _____ Date _____

Math

Generate Equivalent Expressions
Expressions and Equations

DIRECTIONS: Choose or write the correct answer.

> **Strategy** Apply the Commutative, Associative, and Distributive properties to expressions to create equivalent expressions.

> **Test Tip** Review the Commutative, Associative, and Distributive Properties before a test.

1. Write an equivalent expression for the expression $24x + 32y$. Identify the property you used to find an equivalent expression.

$$4(6x + 8y)$$

2. Which expressions are equivalent to $5(3s - 6a)$? Choose all that apply.

- (A) $15s - 30a$
- (B) $3(5s - 10a)$
- (C) $15s - 6a$
- (D) $2(7.5s - 15a)$

3. Write the number of the equivalent expression on the line.

$a(b + c)$ = ____5____ 1) a

$(a + b) + c$ = ____3____ 2) cab

abc = ____2____ 3) $a + (b + c)$

$a(bc)$ = ____4____ 4) $(ab)c$

$a + 0$ = ____1____ 5) $(ab) + (ac)$

4. Which expressions are equivalent to $y + y + y$? Choose all that apply.

- (A) $3y$
- (B) $y3$
- (C) $y + 2y$
- (D) $y2 + y$

5. Quinn had twice as many Twitter followers as Brandon. Today, 8 more people signed up to follow her. Write two equivalent expressions to show the relationship between the number of Quinn's followers and the number of Brandon's followers.

$$2b + 8$$

$$2(b + 4)$$

Identify Equivalent Expressions
Expressions and Equations

DIRECTIONS: Choose or write the correct answer.

Strategy   Use rules, definitions, operations, and properties to solve problems.

1. Sophia wrote the expression $y + y + y$. Aiden told her that the expression $3y$ means the same thing. Is Aiden correct? Why or why not?

_____

_____

_____

_____

2. Choose all of the expressions that are equivalent to $12x$.

Ⓐ $6x + 6x$

Ⓑ $2 (6x)$

Ⓒ $3 (2x + 6)$

Ⓓ $4 \times 3 \times x$

3. Which three expressions from the box are equivalent to $4 (8c + 2d)$? Write them on the lines.

$32c + 8d$	$8c (4 + 2d)$	$2d (8c + 4)$
$8 (4c + d)$	$2 (16c + 4d)$	$4 \times 8c + 2d$

_____

_____

_____

4. Place the symbols = or ≠ in the boxes to show whether the expressions are equivalent.

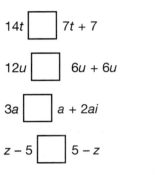

$14t$ ☐ $7t + 7$

$12u$ ☐ $6u + 6u$

$3a$ ☐ $a + 2ai$

$z - 5$ ☐ $5 - z$

Test Tip

The term equivalent means two expressions have the same value, although they are written differently.

5. Write two expressions that are equivalent to $15y + 5$.

_____

_____

Evaluate Equations and Inequalities
Expressions and Equations

DIRECTIONS: Choose or write the correct answer.

> ## Strategy
> Use basic operations and properties to isolate variables and find the value or values of the variables.

1. Choose the value of q that makes the equation true.

$15q - 12 = 18$

- (A) 1
- (B) 2
- (C) 3
- (D) 4

> ## Test Tip
> For multiple choice questions, try each answer choice in the equation or inequality to see which is correct.

2. Choose the value or values of p that makes the inequality true.

$4p + 9 < 25$

- (A) 2
- (B) 4
- (C) 6
- (D) 8

3. Write 3 numbers that can be substituted for f to make the inequality true.

$\frac{1}{2}f - 3 > 7$

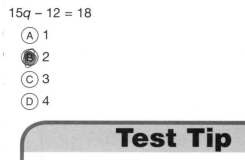

24

48

56

4. Substitute a value for k that makes both the equation and the inequality true.

$2k + 3 = 13 \qquad 3k - 10 < 6$

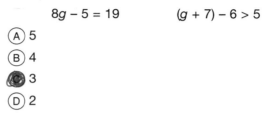

$k = \underline{5}$

5. Which number can be substituted for g to make the equation true but the inequality false?

$8g - 5 = 19 \qquad (g + 7) - 6 > 5$

- (A) 5
- (B) 4
- (C) 3
- (D) 2

6. Write 3 numbers that can be substituted for w to make the inequality true.

$(2w - 5) < 0$

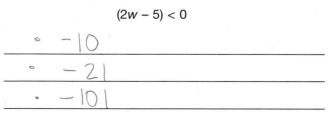

-10

-21

-101

Write Expressions
Expressions and Equations

DIRECTIONS: Choose or write the correct answer.

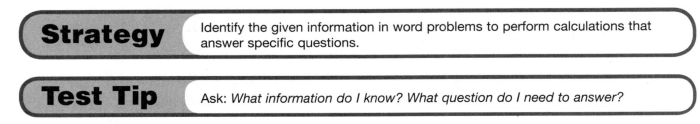

Strategy — Identify the given information in word problems to perform calculations that answer specific questions.

Test Tip — Ask: *What information do I know? What question do I need to answer?*

1. The highway department uses 6 gallons of paint for every 10 blocks of highway stripe. How many gallons will be needed for 250 blocks of highway stripe? Choose the expression that would help you find out.

   (A) $(6 \times 10) + 250 = g$

   (B) $250 - (10 \div 6) = g$

   (C) $250 \times 10 \times 6 = g$

   (D) $(250 \div 10) \times 6 = g$

2. A hiker started out with w ounces of water. She drank 9 ounces of water after hiking 5 miles and 16 more when she reached mile marker 8. She had 31 ounces of water left. How many ounces of water did she start with? Choose the expression that will help you find the answer.

   (A) $w - (9 + 16) = 31$

   (B) $w + (9 - 16) = 31$

   (C) $(16 - 9) + w = 31$

   (D) $w + (9 + 16) = 31$

3. Write an expression that will help you solve this problem: Jackson is training for his track team. He runs m miles each day for 4 days. How many miles will he have run after 6 days?

   _____

4. Emma is buying plastic spoons for the class ice cream party. There are 32 students and teachers in the class. What expression will help Emma know if 4 packs of spoons will be enough if each pack contains s spoons?

   (A) $4 \div s = 32$

   (B) $32 \times 4 = s$

   (C) $4s \leq 32$

   (D) $4s \geq 32$

   Write how you know.

   _____

   _____

   _____

   _____

   _____

5. Ethan has 5 birthday treat bags. He needs to buy more to have enough for his class of 27 students. Treat bags come in packages of 8. Write an expression to show how many packages Ethan should buy.

   _____

Write and Solve Equations
Expressions and Equations

DIRECTIONS: Choose or write the correct answer.

> ### Strategy
> Look for key words in word problems that help you know which operation to use.

1. What is the value of *z* in the equation
   $12 \times z = 144$?

   _____

2. Mr. Smith has 54 books. He wants to store them in a bookcase that has 9 shelves. Write and solve an equation that will help Mr. Smith know how many books to put on each shelf so that they are distributed evenly.

   _____

> ### Test Tip
> Finding how many equal groups or amounts usually indicates a division problem.

3. Olivia bought 17 packages of hair ribbons. Write and solve an equation to find out how many ribbons are in each pack if there are 68 ribbons total.

   _____

> ### Test Tip
> Words such as *total* often indicate addition or multiplication.

4. Harry had a bin of toy cars. He gave away 9 cars and has 54 left. Which equation tells how many cars Harry started with?

   (A) $9 + 54 = c$
   (B) $54 \div 9 = c$
   (C) $c + 54 = 9$
   (D) $c - 9 = 54$

Write another problem that could be solved using the same equation.

_____

_____

_____

_____

_____

5. If $z + 8 = 31$, then $z =$ _____

6. Farmer Ted bought some wire fencing. He put up 325 feet today and saved the last 150 for tomorrow. Which two equations show how many feet of wire fencing Farmer Ted bought?

   (A) $f - 325 = 150$
   (B) $f + 325 = 150$
   (C) $150 + f = 325$
   (D) $325 + 150 = f$

Use Inequalities
Expressions and Equations

DIRECTIONS: Choose or write the correct answer.

Strategy Use number lines to understand and solve inequalities.

Test Tip Remember that an open, or hollow, circle on a number line means the number at that point is not included (less than; greater than). A closed, or filled-in, circle on a number line means the number at that point is included (less than or equal to; greater than or equal to).

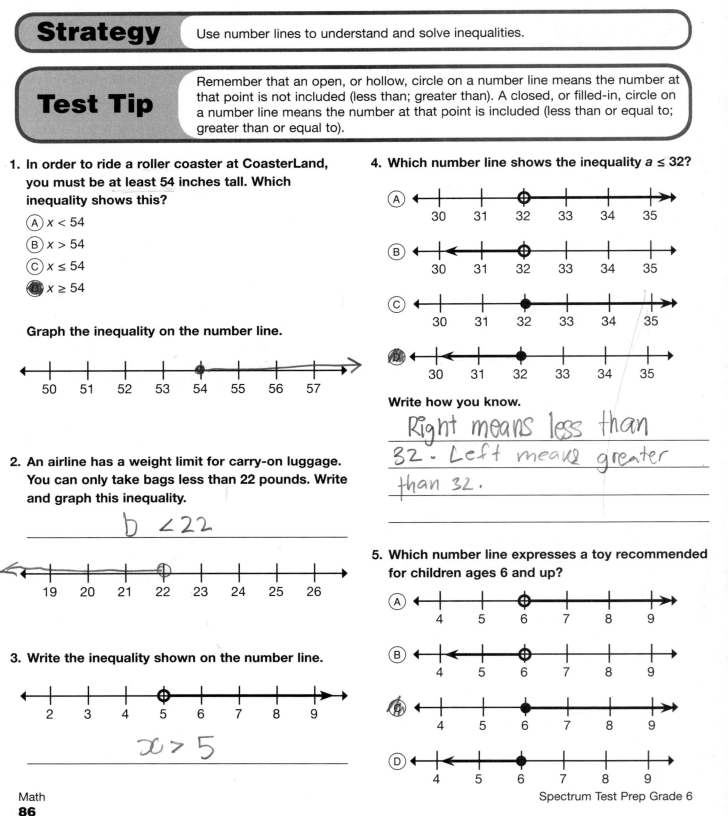

1. **In order to ride a roller coaster at CoasterLand, you must be at least 54 inches tall. Which inequality shows this?**

    (A) $x < 54$

    (B) $x > 54$

    (C) $x \le 54$

    (D) $x \ge 54$

    Graph the inequality on the number line.

2. **An airline has a weight limit for carry-on luggage. You can only take bags less than 22 pounds. Write and graph this inequality.**

    $b < 22$

3. **Write the inequality shown on the number line.**

    $x > 5$

4. **Which number line shows the inequality $a \le 32$?**

    (A) ... (B) ... (C) ... (D)

    Write how you know.

    Right means less than 32. Left means greater than 32.

5. **Which number line expresses a toy recommended for children ages 6 and up?**

    (A) ... (B) ... (C) ... (D)

Name _____ Date 10-7-19

Math

Use Dependent and Independent Variab...
Expressions and Equations

DIRECTIONS: Choose or write the correct answer.

> **Strategy** Use tables and graphs to understand and solve a problem.

1. Mrs. Wacker looked at the chart below to determine how many ounces of chocolate mint sauce she needed to prepare for the vanilla bean pie her guests will enjoy at the dinner party.

Servings (s)	1	2	3	4	5
Ounces of Sauce Needed (n)	2	4	6	8	10

Which equation shows the relationship between the number of servings and the amount of sauce needed?

(A) $n = 2s$
(B) $n = s + 2$
(C) $n = n \div s$
(D) $n = s + 1$

2. The table below shows the relationship between time (t) in hours and distance (d) in miles. Complete the table and write the equation represented by the table.

Time (t)	1	2	3	4
Distance (d)	65	130	195	260

__195, 260__ $d = 65T$

Using the equation you just wrote, determine the distance traveled if t = 10.

650 miles

3. Liam is four years younger than Isabella. Complete the table to show the ages of both children. Then, graph the relationship.

Liam (L)	2	4	10	14
Isabella (I)	6	8	14	18

4. A grocery store always orders twice as many pounds of apples as pounds of pears. Write an equation for this relationship. Then, complete a function table and graph the function.

$p = 2a$ _____

_____

Pears (p)	4	8	12	16
Apples (a)	2	4	6	8

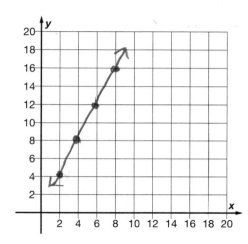

Find Area of Polygons
Geometry

DIRECTIONS: Choose or write the correct answer.

Strategy   Use formulas for area to calculate the area of given figures.

Test Tip   The formula for the area of a rectangle is $A = l \times w$. The formula for the area of a triangle is $\frac{1}{2}(b \times h)$.

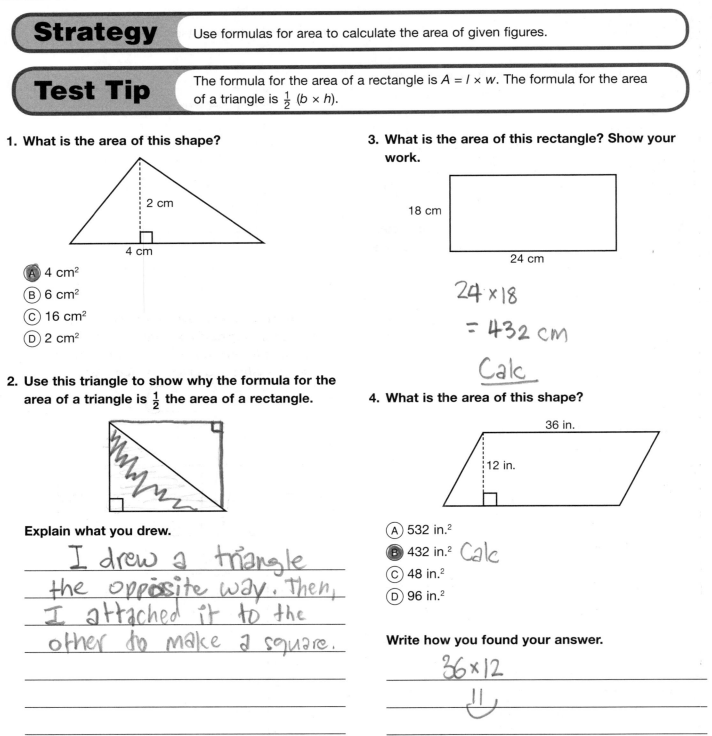

1. What is the area of this shape?

2 cm

4 cm

- (A) 4 cm²
- (B) 6 cm²
- (C) 16 cm²
- (D) 2 cm²

2. Use this triangle to show why the formula for the area of a triangle is $\frac{1}{2}$ the area of a rectangle.

Explain what you drew.

I drew a triangle the opposite way. Then, I attached it to the other to make a square.

3. What is the area of this rectangle? Show your work.

18 cm

24 cm

24 × 18

= 432 cm

Calc

4. What is the area of this shape?

36 in.

12 in.

- (A) 532 in.²
- (B) 432 in.² Calc
- (C) 48 in.²
- (D) 96 in.²

Write how you found your answer.

36 × 12

Find Area of Polygons
Geometry

DIRECTIONS: Choose or write the correct answer.

Strategy   Sketch the shape and label with measurements to understand how to find area.

5. Mason wants to build a fort that fits on the patio. He wants to know what the square footage of the fort will be. The patio is 16 feet long and 9 feet wide. What will the area of the fort's floor be?

   (A) 51 ft.^{2}

   (B) 100 ft.^{2}

   (C) 144 ft.^{2}

   (D) 162 ft.^{2}

6. Mason wants the walls of the fort to be 6 feet high. What will the areas of the walls be?

   (A) 96 ft.^{2} and 54 ft.^{2}

   (B) 30 ft.^{2} and 44 ft.^{2}

   (C) 9 ft.^{2} and 16 ft.^{2}

   (D) 6 ft.^{2}

7. The roof of Mason's fort will have a peak, so he will need to make two triangles. The triangles will go above the 9-foot sides of the fort and will be 2 feet from base to peak. What will the area of each triangle be?

   _____

8. Draw and label a rectangle that has an area of 24 cm^2.

9. Draw and label a rectangle that has an area of 24 cm^2.

Write how you decided on the length and width for your right triangle.

_____

_____

_____

_____

_____

_____

Find Area of Polygons
Geometry

> **Strategy**   Decompose a shape, or break it down into smaller shapes, to find area.

10. A football field is 100 yards long and 50 yards wide. What is the area of a football field?

_____

11. The marching band forms a triangle on the field. The base of the triangle takes up $\frac{1}{2}$ the length of the field, and the peak of the triangle reaches the opposite side of the field. How much area does the marching band's triangle take up?

   Ⓐ 1,250 yd.²

   Ⓑ 5,000 yd.²

   Ⓒ 100 yd.²

   Ⓓ 1,000 yd.²

12. Decompose this shape to find its area.

12 in.   8 in.   6 in.

_____

Write how you found your answer.

_____

_____

_____

_____

_____

_____

_____

13. Draw and label a triangle formed when a rectangle with an area of 60 cm² is cut in half.

Write how you found your answer.

_____

_____

_____

_____

_____

_____

_____

_____

What is the area of the triangle?

_____

14. Draw and label two other triangles that have the same area as the triangle you drew above.

Find Volume of Rectangular Prisms
Geometry

DIRECTIONS: Choose or write the correct answer.

Strategy   Use drawings to understand and find volume.

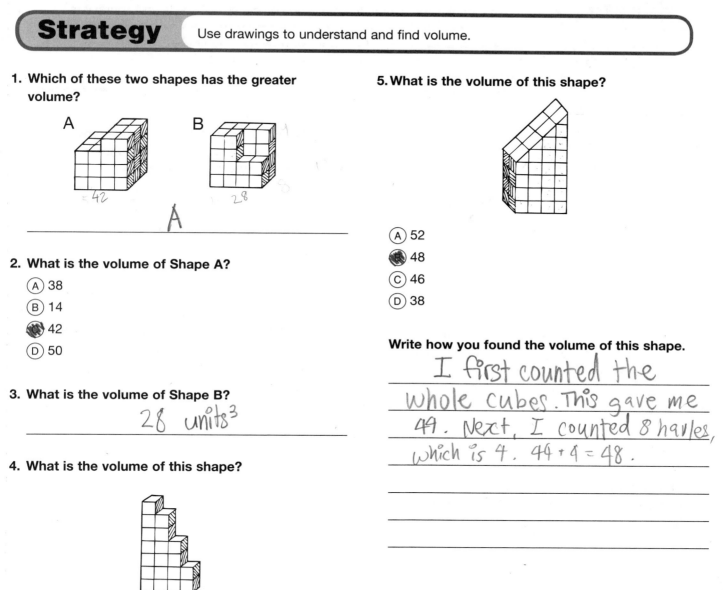

1. Which of these two shapes has the greater volume?

A   B

= 42   28

_____A_____

2. What is the volume of Shape A?

- (A) 38
- (B) 14
- 42
- (D) 50

3. What is the volume of Shape B?

28 units³

_____

4. What is the volume of this shape?

19 units³

_____

5. What is the volume of this shape?

- (A) 52
- 48
- (C) 46
- (D) 38

Write how you found the volume of this shape.

I first counted the whole cubes. This gave me 44. Next, I counted 8 havles, which is 4. 44 + 4 = 48.

Find Volume of Rectangular Prisms
Geometry

> **Strategy**   Use formulas for volume to calculate the volumes of solids and containers.

> **Test Tip**   The formula for the volume of a rectangular prism is $l \times w \times h$, or $B \times h$, where B is the area of the base.

6. Find the volumes of the rectangular prisms. Include the appropriate units in your answer.

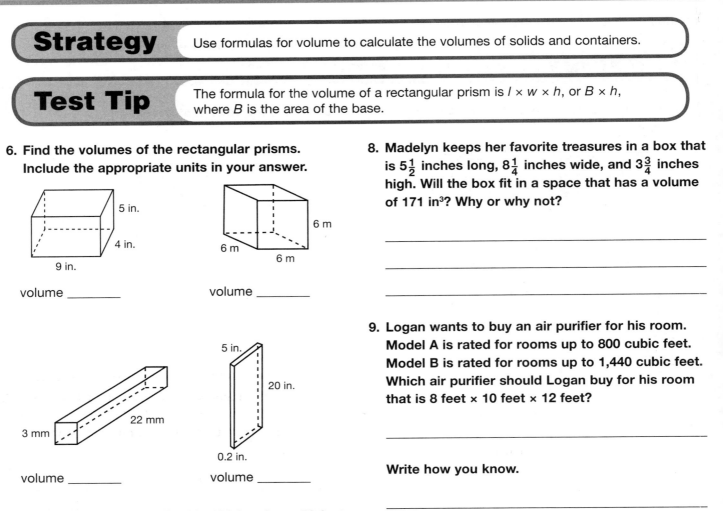

volume _____

volume _____

volume _____

volume _____

7. The Westtown Public Pool is 100 feet long, 50 feet wide, and 5 feet deep. How many cubic feet of water does the pool hold?

(A) 2,500 ft.³

(B) 50,000 ft.³

(C) 25,000 ft.³

(D) 250,000 ft.²

8. Madelyn keeps her favorite treasures in a box that is $5\frac{1}{2}$ inches long, $8\frac{1}{4}$ inches wide, and $3\frac{3}{4}$ inches high. Will the box fit in a space that has a volume of 171 in³? Why or why not?

_____

_____

_____

9. Logan wants to buy an air purifier for his room. Model A is rated for rooms up to 800 cubic feet. Model B is rated for rooms up to 1,440 cubic feet. Which air purifier should Logan buy for his room that is 8 feet × 10 feet × 12 feet?

_____

Write how you know.

_____

_____

_____

_____

10. What is the volume of a box with the dimensions 72 in. × 35 in. × 22 in.?

_____

Draw Polygons in the Coordinate Plane
Geometry

DIRECTIONS: Choose or write the correct answer.

Strategy   Graph data to visualize how numbers can describe two- and three-dimensional figures.

1. Write the ordered pairs for the vertices of the triangle.

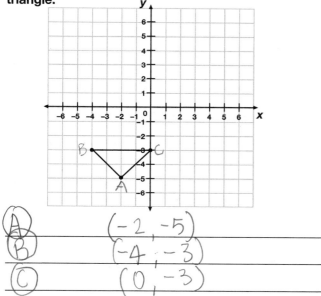

A   (-2, -5)
B   (-4, -3)
C   (0, -3)

2. Write the ordered pairs for the vertices of the rhombus.

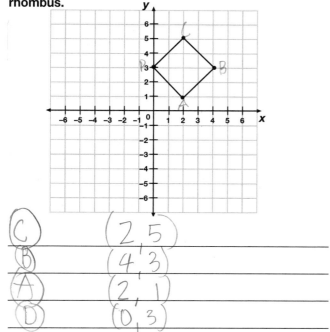

C   (2, 5)
B   (4, 3)
A   (2, 1)
D   (0, 3)

3. Draw a rectangle on the coordinate plane using the following ordered pairs: (2, –3), (6, –3), (6, 3), and (2, 3).

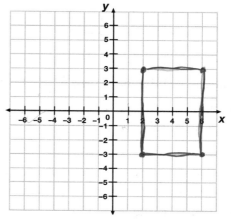

4. Consider the following ordered pairs: (–5, 1), (1, 1), and (0, –5). How can you tell what the shape will be before you start? Plot the points to confirm your answer.

It is an triangle because 3 points, means 3 lines.

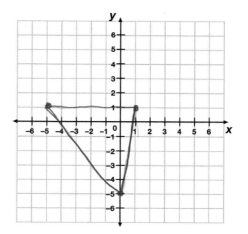

Use Nets
Geometry

DIRECTIONS: Choose or write the correct answer.

> ## Strategy Use drawings to understand and solve a problem.

Use the net to answer Questions 1–3.

6 in.

1. What shape will this net make when it is folded?

  (A) square

  (B) triangular prism

  (C) cube

  (D) cylinder

Write how you know.

_____

_____

_____

_____

2. What is the surface area of this shape?

_____

Write how you know.

_____

_____

_____

_____

_____

3. What is the volume of this shape?

_____

Write how you know.

_____

_____

_____

Use the net to answer questions 4–5.

3 cm   2.6 cm

4. What shape will this net make when it is folded?

_____

5. Write how you can find the surface area of the shape.

_____

_____

_____

_____

Use Nets
Geometry

DIRECTIONS: Choose or write the correct answer.

> **Strategy**   Look at drawings and their labels carefully to understand and solve a problem.

6. Avery is wrapping a gift for her sister. She wants to cut a piece of wrapping paper that will cover the box exactly. The box is shown below. Draw a net that Avery can use as a model for cutting her wrapping paper. Label the measurements she will need.

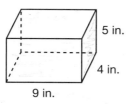

5 in.

4 in.

9 in.

7. Cole went to the store to buy a box to ship a set of books to his friend. He found this box, which he has to put together.

$5\frac{1}{2}$ in.

$8\frac{1}{2}$ in.

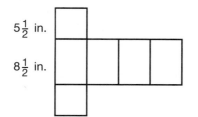

The book set comes in a box with a volume of 258 in.³. Will this box be large enough to ship the books?

_____

Write how you know.

_____

_____

8. How many square feet of paper are needed to cover this pyramid completely with no gaps or overlaps?

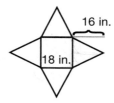

16 in.

18 in.

_____

Recognize Statistical Questions
Statistics and Probability

DIRECTIONS: Choose or write the correct answer.

> **Strategy** Identify the possible answers to a question to determine if it would be useful for gathering statistical data.

1. **Look at the list of questions. If the question is statistical, that is, there will be variability in the answers, then write it in the *Statistical Question* column. If the question is not a statistical question, then write it in the *Nonstatistical Question* column.**

   What is my name? ✓

   How old are students in your class?

   How old am I?

   How much do workers at Company B earn?

   What color shirts are sixth graders wearing?

   What color shirt am I wearing?

   When is my birthday?

   In which month do the most birthdays occur?

Statistical Question	Nonstatistical Question

2. **You are doing a survey to find out about sixth graders' favorite foods. Which are good statistical questions? Choose all that apply.**

   (A) What kinds of food do you most like to eat?

   (B) Which of these is your favorite: pizza or hot dogs?

   (C) What did you eat for dinner last night?

   (D) What is your favorite food?

3. **Jayden stood outside a Mexican restaurant and asked customers going in what their favorite food is. Is this a good way for him to collect statistical data on favorite foods? Explain your answer.**

   _____

   _____

   _____

   _____

4. **What would be the best way to collect data about students' favorite television shows?**

   (A) Ask your three best friends what their favorite shows are.

   (B) Look online to see what the top rated shows are.

   (C) Ask students in your school to participate in a survey.

   (D) Post a question on your social media page.

Analyze Data
Statistics and Probability

DIRECTIONS: Choose or write the correct answer.

Strategy | Organize and display data to interpret them.

Test Tip | *Mean:* average number; *Median:* middle number of ordered data; *Mode:* the value that occurs most often; *Range:* the difference between the largest and smallest values

1. The Sports Store sells soccer goals for the following prices:

$45 $32 $45 $70 $45 $20 $48 $55 $50 $32

Which price best reflects the price of a soccer goal at this store?

(A) maximum: $70

(B) minimum: $20

(C) mean: $44.20

(D) range: $50

2. Super Shoes advertises shoes for "As Low As $20!" Look at the data of the shoe prices at Super Shoes. Do you think $20 is an accurate number for describing the prices at this store? Explain your answer.

$85 $50 $45 $60 $45 $80 $85 $20 $85 $50 $100

No, only 1 shoe is $20.

3. What is the median price of shoes at Super Shoes?

$ 60.0

What is the price range for shoes at Super Shoes?

$ 80

4. Stellar Shoes is just down the block from Super Shoes. They tell customers they sell shoes for "around $35." Is this an accurate description of their prices? Explain your answer.

$35 $40 $35 $25 $75 $50 $63 $80 $42 $35

No, because there is an outlier, 80.

What is the price range for shoes at Stellar Shoes?

$ 45

5. A restaurant offers sandwiches at the following prices: $5.25, $5.50, $6.50, $6.75, $8.00, $6.00, and $4.75. What is the median price of a sandwich?

$ 6.00

What is the price range for sandwiches?

$ 3.25

Math

Understand Measures of Center and Variability
Statistics and Probability

DIRECTIONS: Choose or write the correct answer.

> ## Strategy
> Use measures of center to evaluate data and make decisions.

Use the data in the soccer balls to complete items 1–4. Find the mean, median, mode, and range for each data set.

1. Store 1 Prices

$45 $32
$45 $70 $45
$20 $48 $55
$50 $32

Mean: _____

Median: _____

Mode: _____

Range: _____

2. Store 2 Prices

$35 $40
$35 $25 $75
$50 $63 $80
$42 $35

Mean: _____

Median: _____

Mode: _____

Range: _____

3. Store 3 Prices

$85 $50 $45
$60 $45 $80
$85 $20 $85
$50 $100

Mean: _____

Median: _____

Mode: _____

Range: _____

4. Store 4 Prices

$55 $60
$88 $60 $32
$80 $48 $64
$80 $60

Mean: _____

Median: _____

Mode: _____

Range: _____

5. Store 3 claims they have shoes to fit any budget because they have the largest range of prices. Look at the data for Store 3. Do you agree they have the best variety of prices? Explain your answer.

_____

_____

_____

_____

6. Which store has the lowest average price?

_____

7. If you wanted to find the store with the best variety of low-priced shoes, which would you choose? Which "middle number" could help you make this decision?

_____

_____

_____

Display Data
Statistics and Probability

DIRECTIONS: Choose or write the correct answer.

Strategy   Organize and display data in a variety of ways, then use the graph, plot, or table to interpret the data.

1. Look at the dot plot below.

North Coast California: Number of Earthquakes per Year

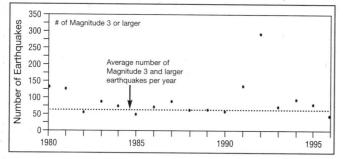

What is this data showing?

(A) strength of earthquakes in California

(B) number of earthquakes per year in California

(C) locations of earthquakes in California

(D) number of deaths from earthquakes per year in California

2. In what year did the greatest number of earthquakes occur?

_____1992_____

3. Based on the data, what is an average number of earthquakes per year on the north coast of California?

(A) about 250

(B) about 150

(C) about 100

(D) about 50

4. The data below represent the dollar sales (in millions) of 29 furniture stores in the state of Kentucky. You want to compare numbers of companies that make from \$22.1 to \$24.1 million; from \$24.2 to 26.1 million; from \$26.2 to 28.1 million, etc. Create a histogram for this purpose.

32.1	27.4	27.8	61.8	27.8	27.0
38.9	24.1	36.6	34.6	24.9	27.3
42.1	28.5	27.1	42.9	36.7	25.2
25.9	27.1	34.2	28.0	34.1	56.5
45.8	28.5	28.4	25.5	40.9	

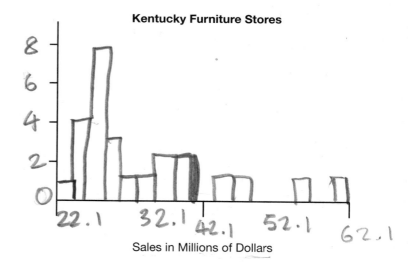

Kentucky Furniture Stores

Sales in Millions of Dollars

Display Data
Statistics and Probability

DIRECTIONS: Choose or write the correct answer.

> **Strategy** Represent data using a box-and-whisker plot in order to interpret it in useful ways.

A company wants to know how far its employees commute for work each day. They asked their employees to tell them how many miles they travel one way each day. The data is listed below.

1   5   2   14   11   8   2   4   1   13   10   6   5   12
2   3   11   12   14   10   5   6   7   1   12   5   16

5. To find the median distance traveled and the spread of the distances traveled, the company is going to plot the data in a box-and-whisker plot. First, order the data from least to greatest.

_____

_____

_____

6. What is the median number in the data?

_____

7. What is the median of the lower half of the numbers?

_____

What is the median of the upper half of the numbers?

_____

8. Draw a box-and-whisker plot using the data and center points you have found.

Name _____ Date _____

Math

Summarize Data
Statistics and Probability

DIRECTIONS: Choose or write the correct answer.

 **Strategy**   Differentiate among various ways of representing data to determine the best choice for a given data set.

Use the histogram to answer items 1–3.

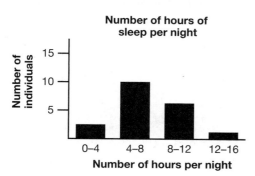

Number of hours of sleep per night

Number of individuals

Number of hours per night

1. **What does this data show?**

   (A) number of hours people sleep each night

   (B) number of people who sleep 8 hours every night

   (C) percent of people who sleep 10 or more hours each night

   (D) what time people wake up in the morning

2. **Why is a histogram a good way to display the data?**

   _____

   _____

   _____

3. **Summarize the data from the histogram.**

   _____

   _____

   _____

   _____

4. **Can you tell from this graph how many people were surveyed about their sleeping habits? Explain.**

   _____

   _____

   _____

   _____

   _____

   _____

5. **Summarize the data you plotted in the box-and-whisker plot on page 100.**

   _____

   _____

   _____

   _____

6. **Can you tell from the employee commuting data how many people were surveyed? Explain.**

   _____

   _____

   _____

   _____

Strategy Review

Strategy   Apply prior knowledge and basic operations to solve problems.

EXAMPLE

Mary is catering a party. She made $15\frac{1}{2}$ pounds of cheesy potatoes. She wants her servers to put $\frac{1}{8}$ pound on each plate. How many servings of cheesy potatoes will she have?

First, write an expression to model the problem.

$15\frac{1}{2} \div \frac{1}{8}$

Next, use the process for dividing fractions to evaluate the expression.

$15\frac{1}{2} = \frac{31}{2}$

$\frac{31}{2} \div \frac{1}{8} = \frac{31}{2} \times \frac{8}{1}$

$\frac{31}{2} \times \frac{8}{1} = \frac{248}{2}$

Simplify: $\frac{248}{2} = 124$

Mary will have 124 servings of cheesy potatoes.

1. Nash Park has an area of $\frac{3}{4}$ square miles. One side of the park is $\frac{1}{2}$ mile. How long is the other side of the park? Write and evaluate an expression to answer the question.

_____

How did the strategy help you answer the question?

_____

_____

_____

EXAMPLE

A swimming instructor wants to know the age spread of the students in his classes. He asks his students to tell him how old they are. The data is shown below.

5 7 12 4 9 18 13 11 4 7 11 10 6 15 7 8 14
12 9 10 6 4 12

Make a box-and-whisker plot to analyze the data.

First, order the ages from lowest to highest

4 4 4 5 6 6 7 7 7 8 9 9 10 10 11 11 12 12
12 13 14 15 18

Then, find the median of the data.

4 4 4 5 6 6 7 7 7 8 9 9 10 10 11 11 12 12
12 13 14 15 18

Next, find the medians of the lower and upper sets.

4 4 4 5 6 6 7 7 7 8 9 9 10 10 11 11 12 12
12 13 14 15 18

Finally, use your data points to make your box-and-whisker plot.

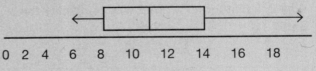

0   2   4   6   8   10   12   14   16   18

Now, you can use your box-and-whisker plot to answer questions about the data.

2. How many people are taking swimming lessons?

_____

3. What is the median age of the students? _____

4. What is the age span of the majority of the students?

_____

Strategy Review

Strategy — Look for key words in word problems that help you determine which operation to use.

EXAMPLE

Julio is ordering meat for his restaurant. He orders 15.75 pounds of ground beef at $1.89 per pound, 20 pounds of pork at $3.79 per pound, and 25.5 pounds of steak at $5.25 per pound. He has a $50 credit with the meat distributor. How much will Julio have to pay for his order?

First, identify key words that tell you what operations to use.

The word "per" suggests multiplication.

The word "credit" suggests subtraction.

Looking for how much someone has to pay suggests addition.

Then, write an expression to represent the situation.

$[(15.75 \times 1.89) + (20 \times 3.79) + (25.5 \times 5.25)] - 50$

Evaluate parentheses. Since the numbers are in the context of money, round to the nearest hundredth.

$(15.75 \times 1.89) = 29.77$

$(20 \times 3.79) = 75.80$

$(25.5 \times 5.25) = 133.88$

Complete the operations within the square brackets.

$[29.77 + 75.80 + 133.88] = 239.45$

Add or subtract from left to right.

$239.45 - 50 = 189.45$

Julio has to pay $189.45

(B) $4.97

(C) 4 pounds

(D) $9.67

2. Staci went shopping for new clothes. She bought 3 pairs of jeans. The jeans were on sale for $35.99 each, and she had a coupon for buy two, get one free. How much did Staci spend on new jeans?

(A) $107.97

(B) $71.98

(C) $35.99

(D) 143.96

Strategy

Use drawings, graphs, or number lines to understand and solve a problem.

3. A movie is rated PG–13. Write and graph an inequality that shows how old you must be to see this movie without a parent.

$a \geq 13$

1. Katie bought a $\frac{1}{2}$ pound of bananas for $1.29 per pound, $1\frac{1}{2}$ pounds of grapes at $0.89 per pound, and 2 pounds of cherries at $1.49 per pound. How much did Katie spend on her fruit?

(A) $3.67

Strategy Review

Strategy Write and solve an equation to solve a real-world problem.

EXAMPLE

Charlie tracked how long it took to fill the baby pool for his little sister. He measured the water every five minutes and tracked it in the table below. Charlie wants to know how long it would take to fill the pool to its full 48 inches.

Time (t) in minutes	1	2	3	4	5
Water height (h) in inches	6	12	18	24	30

First, write an equation that represents the relationship between the two variables.

$t \times 6 = h$

Next, solve the equation to answer the question.

$t \times 6 = 48$

$t = 8$

It would take 8 minutes to fill the pool completely.

1. Ethan made up a game in which a player earns 7 points for every goal scored. He wants to know how many goals will be needed to earn 84 points. Which equation will give Ethan his answer?

   (A) $84 \times g = 7$

   (B) $7 \div g = 84$

   (C) $7 + g = 84$

   (D) $7 \times g = 84$

2. Carson is 3 years older than his sister. How old will Carson be when his sister is 42?

Complete the table and write an equation.

sister (s)	1	2	3	4	5
Carson (c)					

_____

Strategy

Read word problems carefully to identify the given information and the question.

3. At 9:00, Mrs. Rhodes asked her class to complete a survey. She learned that $\frac{2}{3}$ of her class prefers to learn through technology. She also learned the $\frac{3}{4}$ of the students who said they prefer to learn through technology were girls. What fraction of the students who said they prefer to learn through technology were boys?

What is the given information?

_____

_____

_____

_____

What are you being asked to find?

_____

_____

_____

Is any of the given information extra, or not needed?

_____

_____

_____

Strategy Review

> **Strategy**   Use rules, properties, or formulas to solve problems.

EXAMPLE

Cleo received a package in the mail that came in a $12\frac{3}{4}$ in. by $13\frac{1}{4}$ in. by $7\frac{1}{2}$ in box. Use the formula for volume, $V = l \times w \times h$ or $V = Bh$, to find the volume of the carton.

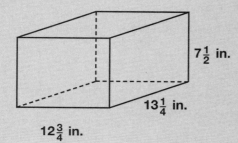

$7\frac{1}{2}$ in.

$13\frac{1}{4}$ in.

$12\frac{3}{4}$ in.

First, write the formula for the volume of a right rectangular prism.

$V = l \times w \times h$

Put the measurements into the formula.

$V = l \times w \times h = 12\frac{3}{4} \times 13\frac{1}{4} \times 7\frac{1}{2} = \frac{40,545}{32} = 1,267\frac{1}{32}$

The volume of the box is $1,267\frac{1}{32}$ in.³

1. Ana has a recipe box that her grandmother gave her. It is $3\frac{1}{2}$ inches tall, $6\frac{1}{4}$ long, and $4\frac{1}{4}$ inches wide. What is the volume of the recipe box?

_____

2. Haddon is painting his wall. The wall is $10\frac{3}{4}$ feet long and $8\frac{1}{2}$ feet high. What is the area that Hudson will be painting?

  Ⓐ $91\frac{4}{7}$ ft.²

  Ⓑ $91\frac{3}{8}$ ft.²

  Ⓒ $91\frac{375}{8}$ ft.²

  Ⓓ 92 ft.²

3. Haddon wants to put a border all around his room. If all of Haddon's walls are the same dimensions, how long must the border be to fit all the way around the room?

  Ⓐ $10\frac{3}{4}$ feet

  Ⓑ $42\frac{3}{4}$ feet

  Ⓒ 43 feet

  Ⓓ 50 feet

4. A fish tank in the shape of a rectangular prism was 24 in. by 36 in. by 18 in. Find the volume of the tank. Show your work.

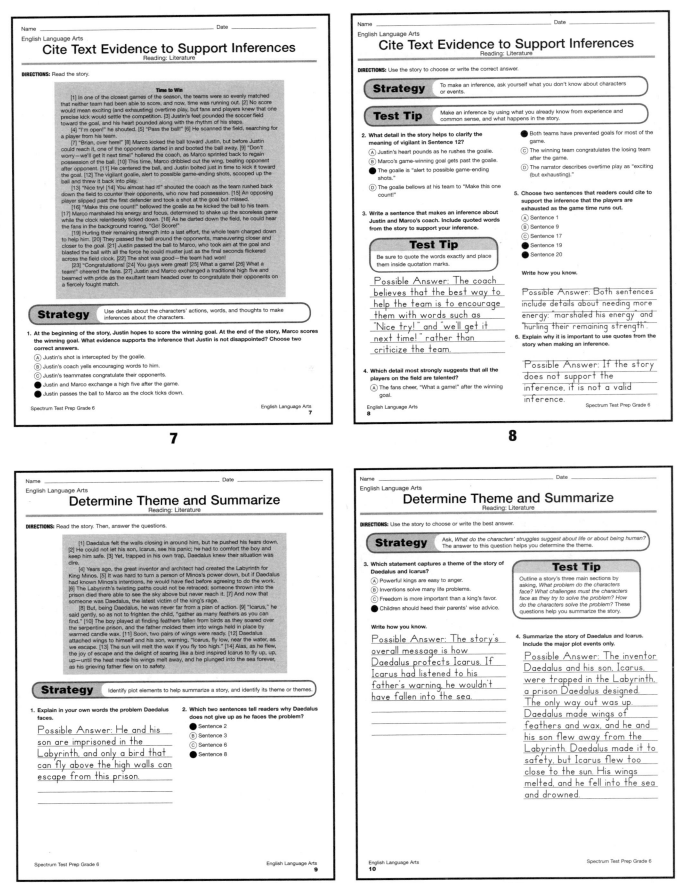

Page 7

Cite Text Evidence to Support Inferences
Reading: Literature

DIRECTIONS: Read the story.

Time to Win

[1] In one of the closest games of the season, the teams were so evenly matched that neither team had been able to score, and now, time was running out. [2] No score would mean exciting (and exhausting) overtime play, but fans and players knew that one precise kick would settle the competition. [3] Justin's feet pounded the soccer field toward the goal, and his heart pounded along with the rhythm of his steps.

[4] "I'm open!" he shouted. [5] "Pass the ball!" [6] He scanned the field, searching for a player from his team.

[7] "Brian, over here!" [8] Marco kicked the ball toward Justin, but before Justin could reach it, one of the opponents darted in and booted the ball away. [9] "Don't worry—we'll get it next time!" hollered the coach, as Marco sprinted back to regain possession of the ball. [10] This time, Marco dribbled out the wing, beating opponent after opponent. [11] He centered the ball, and Justin bolted just in time to kick it toward the goal. [12] The vigilant goalie, alert to possible game-ending shots, scooped up the ball and threw it back into play.

[13] "Nice try! [14] You almost had it!" shouted the coach as the team rushed back down the field to counter their opponents, who now had possession. [15] An opposing player slipped past the first defender and took a shot at the goal but missed. [16] "Make this one count!" bellowed the goalie as he kicked the ball to his team. [17] Marco marshaled his energy and focus, determined to shake up the scoreless game while the clock relentlessly ticked down. [18] As he darted down the field, he could hear the fans in the background roaring, "Go! Score!"

[19] Hurling their remaining strength into a last effort, the whole team charged down to help him. [20] They passed the ball around the opponents, maneuvering closer and closer to the goal. [21] Justin passed the ball to Marco, who took aim at the goal and blasted the ball with all the force he could muster just as the final seconds flickered across the field clock. [22] The shot was good—the team had won!

[23] "Congratulations! [24] You guys were great! [25] What a game! [26] What a team!" cheered the fans. [27] Justin and Marco exchanged a traditional high five and beamed with pride as the exultant team headed over to congratulate their opponents on a fiercely fought match.

Strategy
Use details about the characters' actions, words, and thoughts to make inferences about the characters.

1. At the beginning of the story, Justin hopes to score the winning goal. At the end of the story, Marco scores the winning goal. What evidence supports the inference that Justin is not disappointed? Choose two correct answers.
   - (A) Justin's shot is intercepted by the goalie.
   - (B) Justin's coach yells encouraging words to him.
   - (C) Justin's teammates congratulate their opponents.
   - ● Justin and Marco exchange a high five after the game.
   - ● Justin passes the ball to Marco as the clock ticks down.

7

Page 8

Cite Text Evidence to Support Inferences
Reading: Literature

DIRECTIONS: Use the story to choose or write the correct answer.

Strategy
To make an inference, ask yourself what you don't know about characters or events.

Test Tip
Make an inference by using what you already know from experience and common sense, and what happens in the story.

2. What detail in the story helps to clarify the meaning of vigilant in Sentence 12?
   - (A) Justin's heart pounds as he rushes the goalie.
   - (B) Marco's game-winning goal gets past the goalie.
   - ● The goalie is "alert to possible game-ending shots."
   - (D) The goalie bellows at his team to "Make this one count!"

3. Write a sentence that makes an inference about Justin and Marco's coach. Include quoted words from the story to support your inference.

Test Tip
Be sure to quote the words exactly and place them inside quotation marks.

Possible Answer: The coach believes that the best way to help the team is to encourage them with words such as "Nice try!" and "we'll get it next time!" rather than criticize the team.

4. Which detail most strongly suggests that all the players on the field are talented?
   - (A) The fans cheer, "What a game!" after the winning goal.

   - ● Both teams have prevented goals for most of the game.
   - (C) The winning team congratulates the losing team after the game.
   - (D) The narrator describes overtime play as "exciting (but exhausting)."

5. Choose two sentences that readers could cite to support the inference that the players are exhausted as the game time runs out.
   - (A) Sentence 1
   - (B) Sentence 9
   - (C) Sentence 17
   - ● Sentence 19
   - ● Sentence 20

   Write how you know.

   Possible Answer: Both sentences include details about needing more energy: "marshaled his energy" and "hurling their remaining strength".

6. Explain why it is important to use quotes from the story when making an inference.

   Possible Answer: If the story does not support the inference, it is not a valid inference.

8

Page 9

Determine Theme and Summarize
Reading: Literature

DIRECTIONS: Read the story. Then, answer the questions.

[1] Daedalus felt the walls closing in around him, but he pushed his fears down. [2] He could not let his son, Icarus, see his panic; he had to comfort the boy and keep him safe. [3] Yet, trapped in his own trap, Daedalus knew their situation was dire.

[4] Years ago, the great inventor and architect had created the Labyrinth for King Minos. [5] It was hard to turn a person of Minos's power down, but if Daedalus had known Minos's intentions, he would have fled before agreeing to do the work. [6] The Labyrinth's twisting paths could not be retraced; someone thrown into the prison died there able to see the sky but never reach it. [7] And now that someone was Daedalus, the latest victim of the king's rage.

[8] But, being Daedalus, he was never far from a plan of action. [9] "Icarus," he said gently, so as not to frighten the child, "gather as many feathers as you can find." [10] The boy played at finding feathers fallen from birds as they soared over the serpentine prison, and the father molded them into wings held in place by warmed candle wax. [11] Soon, two pairs of wings were ready. [12] Daedalus attached wings to himself and his son, warning, "Icarus, fly low, near the water, as we escape. [13] The sun will melt the wax if you fly too high." [14] Alas, as he flew, the joy of escape and the delight of soaring like a bird inspired Icarus to fly up, up, up—until the heat made his wings melt away, and he plunged into the sea forever, as his grieving father flew on to safety.

Strategy
Identify plot elements to help summarize a story, and identify its theme or themes.

1. Explain in your own words the problem Daedalus faces.

   Possible Answer: He and his son are imprisoned in the Labyrinth, and only a bird that can fly above the high walls can escape from this prison.

2. Which two sentences tell readers why Daedalus does not give up as he faces the problem?
   - ● Sentence 2
   - (B) Sentence 3
   - (C) Sentence 6
   - ● Sentence 8

9

Page 10

Determine Theme and Summarize
Reading: Literature

DIRECTIONS: Use the story to choose or write the best answer.

Strategy
Ask, What do the characters' struggles suggest about life or about being human? The answer to this question helps you determine the theme.

3. Which statement captures a theme of the story of Daedalus and Icarus?
   - (A) Powerful kings are easy to anger.
   - (B) Inventions solve many life problems.
   - (C) Freedom is more important than a king's favor.
   - ● Children should heed their parents' wise advice.

   Write how you know.

   Possible Answer: The story's overall message is how Daedalus protects Icarus. If Icarus had listened to his father's warning, he wouldn't have fallen into the sea.

Test Tip
Outline a story's three main sections by asking, What problem do the characters face? What challenges must the characters face as they try to solve the problem? How do the characters solve the problem? These questions help you summarize the story.

4. Summarize the story of Daedalus and Icarus. Include the major plot events only.

   Possible Answer: The inventor Daedalus and his son, Icarus, were trapped in the Labyrinth, a prison Daedalus designed. The only way out was up. Daedalus made wings of feathers and wax, and he and his son flew away from the Labyrinth. Daedalus made it to safety, but Icarus flew too close to the sun. His wings melted, and he fell into the sea and drowned.

10

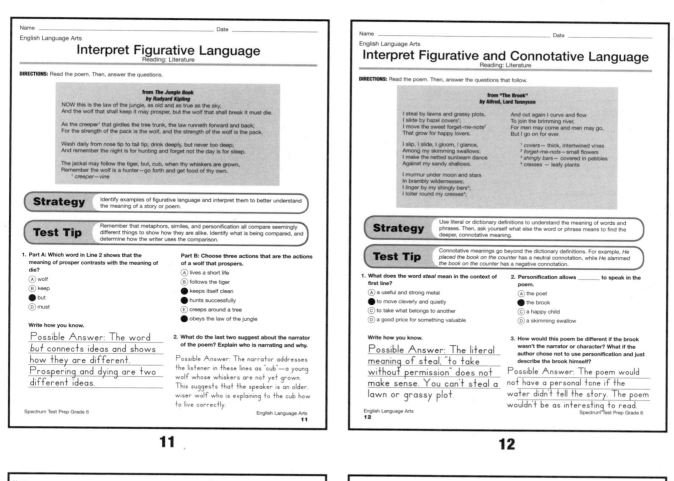

Name _____ **Date** _____

English Language Arts

Interpret Figurative Language
Reading: Literature

DIRECTIONS: Read the poem. Then, answer the questions.

> **from *The Jungle Book***
> **by Rudyard Kipling**
> NOW this is the law of the jungle, as old and as true as the sky,
> And the wolf that shall keep it may prosper, but the wolf that shall break it must die.
>
> As the creeper¹ that girdles the tree trunk, the law runneth forward and back;
> For the strength of the pack is the wolf, and the strength of the wolf is the pack.
>
> Wash daily from nose tip to tail tip; drink deeply, but never too deep;
> And remember the night is for hunting and forget not the day is for sleep.
>
> The jackal may follow the tiger, but, cub, when thy whiskers are grown,
> Remember the wolf is a hunter—go forth and get food of thy own.
> ¹ *creeper—vine*

Strategy — Identify examples of figurative language and interpret them to better understand the meaning of a story or poem.

Test Tip — Remember that metaphors, similes, and personification all compare seemingly different things to show how they are alike. Identify what is being compared, and determine how the writer uses the comparison.

1. **Part A: Which word in Line 2 shows that the meaning of *die* contrasts with the meaning of *prosper*?**
   (A) wolf
   (B) keep
   ● but
   (D) must

Write how you know.

Possible Answer: The word *but* connects ideas and shows how they are different. Prospering and dying are two different ideas.

Part B: Choose three actions that are the actions of a wolf that prospers.
   (A) lives a short life
   (B) follows the tiger
   ● keeps itself clean
   ● hunts successfully
   (E) creeps around a tree
   ● obeys the law of the jungle

2. **What do the last two suggest about the narrator of the poem? Explain who is narrating and why.**

Possible Answer: The narrator addresses the listener in these lines as "cub"—a young wolf whose whiskers are not yet grown. This suggests that the speaker is an older, wiser wolf who is explaining to the cub how to live correctly.

Name _____ **Date** _____

English Language Arts

Interpret Figurative and Connotative Language
Reading: Literature

DIRECTIONS: Read the poem. Then, answer the questions that follow.

> **from "The Brook"**
> **by Alfred, Lord Tennyson**
>
> I steal by lawns and grassy plots,
> I slide by hazel covers¹;
> I move the sweet forget-me-nots²
> That grow for happy lovers.
>
> I slip, I slide, I gloom, I glance,
> Among my skimming swallows,
> I make the netted sunbeam dance
> Against my sandy shallows.
>
> I murmur under moon and stars
> In brambly wildernesses;
> I linger by my shingly bars³;
> I loiter round my cresses⁴
>
> And out again I curve and flow
> To join the brimming river,
> For men may come and men may go,
> But I go on for ever.
>
> ¹ covers— thick, intertwined vines
> ² forget-me-nots—small flowers
> ³ shingly bars— covered in pebbles
> ⁴ cresses — leafy plants

Strategy — Use literal or dictionary definitions to understand the meaning of words and phrases. Then, ask yourself what else the word or phrase means to find the deeper, connotative meaning.

Test Tip — Connotative meanings go beyond the dictionary definitions. For example, *He placed the book on the counter* has a neutral connotation, while *He slammed the book on the counter* has a negative connotation.

1. **What does the word *steal* mean in the context of first line?**
   (A) a useful and strong metal
   ● to move cleverly and quietly
   (C) to take what belongs to another
   (D) a good price for something valuable

Write how you know.

Possible Answer: The literal meaning of steal, "to take without permission" does not make sense. You can't steal a lawn or grassy plot.

2. **Personification allows _____ to speak in the poem.**
   (A) the poet
   ● the brook
   (C) a happy child
   (D) a skimming swallow

3. **How would this poem be different if the brook wasn't the narrator or character? What if the author chose not to use personification and just describe the brook himself?**

Possible Answer: The poem would not have a personal tone if the water didn't tell the story. The poem wouldn't be as interesting to read.

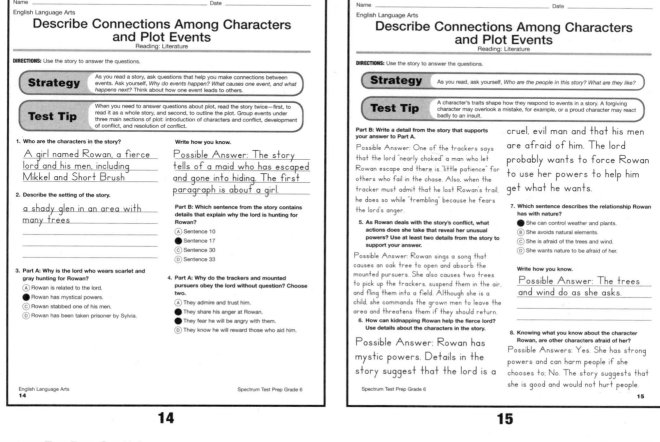

Name _____ **Date** _____

English Language Arts

Describe Connections Among Characters and Plot Events
Reading: Literature

DIRECTIONS: Use the story to answer the questions.

Strategy — As you read a story, ask questions that help you make connections between events. Ask yourself, *Why do events happen? What causes one event, and what happens next?* Think about how one event leads to others.

Test Tip — When you need to answer questions about plot, read the story twice—first, to read it as a whole story, and second, to outline the plot. Group events under three main sections of plot: introduction of characters and conflict, development of conflict, and resolution of conflict.

1. **Who are the characters in the story?**

A girl named Rowan, a fierce lord and his men, including Mikkel and Short Brush

2. **Describe the setting of the story.**

a shady glen in an area with many trees

3. **Part A: Why is the lord who wears scarlet and gray hunting for Rowan?**
   (A) Rowan is related to the lord.
   ● Rowan has mystical powers.
   (C) Rowan stabbed one of his men.
   (D) Rowan has been taken prisoner by Sylvia.

Write how you know.

Possible Answer: The story tells of a maid who has escaped and gone into hiding. The first paragraph is about a girl.

Part B: Which sentence from the story contains details that explain why the lord is hunting for Rowan?
   (A) Sentence 10
   ● Sentence 17
   (C) Sentence 30
   (D) Sentence 33

4. **Part A: Why do the trackers and mounted pursuers obey the lord without question? Choose two.**
   (A) They admire and trust him.
   ● They share his anger at Rowan.
   ● They fear he will be angry with them.
   (D) They know he will reward those who aid him.

Name _____ **Date** _____

English Language Arts

Describe Connections Among Characters and Plot Events
Reading: Literature

DIRECTIONS: Use the story to answer the questions.

Strategy — As you read, ask yourself, *Who are the people in this story? What are they like?*

Test Tip — A character's traits shape how they respond to events in a story. A forgiving character may overlook a mistake, for example, or a proud character may react badly to an insult.

Part B: Write a detail from the story that supports your answer to Part A.

Possible Answer: One of the trackers says that the lord "nearly choked" a man who let Rowan escape and there is "little patience" for others who fail in the chase. Also, when the tracker must admit that he lost Rowan's trail, he does so while "trembling" because he fears the lord's anger.

5. **When Rowan deals with the story's conflict, what actions does she take that reveal her unusual powers? Use at least two details from the story to support your answer.**

Possible Answer: Rowan sings a song that causes an oak tree to open and absorb the mounted pursuers. She also causes two trees to pick up the trackers, suspend them in the air, and fling them into a field. Although she is a child, she commands the grown men to leave the area and threatens them if they should return.

6. **How can kidnapping Rowan help the fierce lord? Use details about the characters in the story.**

Possible Answer: Rowan has mystic powers. Details in the story suggest that the lord is a cruel, evil man and that his men are afraid of him. The lord probably wants to force Rowan to use her powers to help him get what he wants.

7. **Which sentence describes the relationship Rowan has with nature?**
   ● She can control weather and plants.
   (B) She avoids natural elements.
   (C) She is afraid of the trees and wind.
   (D) She wants nature to be afraid of her.

Write how you know.

Possible Answer: The trees and wind do as she asks.

8. **Knowing what you know about the character Rowan, are other characters afraid of her?**

Possible Answers: Yes. She has strong powers and can harm people if she chooses to; No. The story suggests that she is good and would not hurt people.

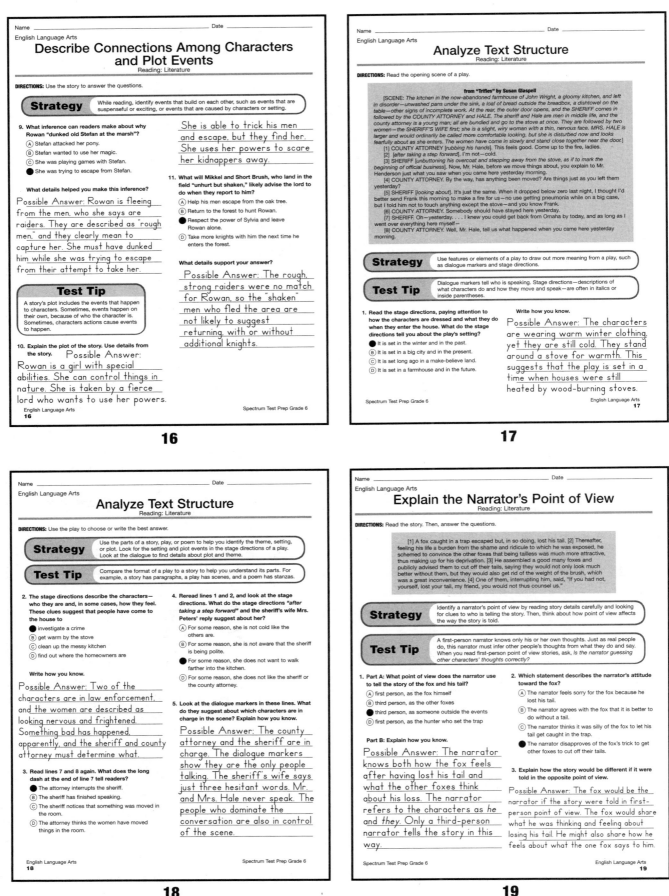

Page 16

Describe Connections Among Characters and Plot Events
Reading: Literature

DIRECTIONS: Use the story to answer the questions.

Strategy While reading, identify events that build on each other, such as events that are suspenseful or exciting, or events that are caused by characters or setting.

9. What inference can readers make about why Rowan "dunked old Stefan at the marsh"?
   - (A) Stefan attacked her pony.
   - (B) Stefan wanted to use her magic.
   - (C) She was playing games with Stefan.
   - ● She was trying to escape from Stefan.

What details helped you make this inference?

Possible Answer: Rowan is fleeing from the men, who she says are raiders. They are described as "rough men," and they clearly mean to capture her. She must have dunked him while she was trying to escape from their attempt to take her.

Test Tip
A story's plot includes the events that happen to characters. Sometimes, events happen on their own, because of who the character is. Sometimes, characters actions cause events to happen.

10. Explain the plot of the story. Use details from the story. Possible Answer: Rowan is a girl with special abilities. She can control things in nature. She is taken by a fierce lord who wants to use her powers.

She is able to trick his men and escape, but they find her. She uses her powers to scare her kidnappers away.

11. What will Mikkel and Short Brush, who land in the field "unhurt but shaken," likely advise the lord to do when they report to him?
   - (A) Help his men escape from the oak tree.
   - (B) Return to the forest to hunt Rowan.
   - ● Respect the power of Sylvia and leave Rowan alone.
   - (D) Take more knights with him the next time he enters the forest.

What details support your answer?

Possible Answer: The rough, strong raiders were no match for Rowan, so the "shaken" men who fled the area are not likely to suggest returning, with or without additional knights.

Page 17

Analyze Text Structure
Reading: Literature

DIRECTIONS: Read the opening scene of a play.

from "Trifles" by Susan Glaspell
[SCENE: The kitchen in the now-abandoned farmhouse of John Wright, a gloomy kitchen, and left in disorder—unwashed pans under the sink, a loaf of bread outside the breadbox, a dishtowel on the table—other signs of incomplete work. At the rear, the outer door opens, and the SHERIFF comes in followed by the COUNTY ATTORNEY and HALE. The sheriff and Hale are men in middle life, and the county attorney is a young man; all are bundled up and go to the stove at once. They are followed by two women—the SHERIFF'S WIFE first; she is a slight, wiry woman with a thin, nervous face. MRS. HALE is larger and would ordinarily be called more comfortable looking, but she is disturbed now and looks fearfully about as she enters. The women have come in slowly and stand close together near the door.]
[1] COUNTY ATTORNEY [rubbing his hands]. This feels good. Come up to the fire, ladies.
[2] [after taking a step forward]. I'm not—cold.
[3] SHERIFF [unbuttoning his overcoat and stepping away from the stove, as if to mark the beginning of official business]. Now, Mr. Hale, before we move things about, you explain to Mr. Henderson just what you saw when you came here yesterday morning.
[4] COUNTY ATTORNEY. By the way, has anything been moved? Are things just as you left them yesterday?
[5] SHERIFF [looking about]. It's just the same. When it dropped below zero last night, I thought I'd better send Frank this morning to make a fire for us—no use getting pneumonia while on a big case, but I told him not to touch anything except the stove—and you know Frank.
[6] COUNTY ATTORNEY. Somebody should have stayed here yesterday.
[7] SHERIFF. Oh—yesterday. . . . I knew you could get back from Omaha by today, and as long as I went over everything here myself—
[8] COUNTY ATTORNEY. Well, Mr. Hale, tell us what happened when you came here yesterday morning.

Strategy Use features or elements of a play to draw out more meaning from a play, such as dialogue markers and stage directions.

Test Tip Dialogue markers tell who is speaking. Stage directions—descriptions of what characters do and how they move and speak—are often in italics or inside parentheses.

1. Read the stage directions, paying attention to how the characters are dressed and what they do when they enter the house. What do the stage directions tell you about the play's setting?
   - ● It is set in the winter and in the past.
   - (B) It is set in a big city and in the present.
   - (C) It is set long ago in a make-believe land.
   - (D) It is set in a farmhouse and in the future.

Write how you know.

Possible Answer: The characters are wearing warm winter clothing, yet they are still cold. They stand around a stove for warmth. This suggests that the play is set in a time when houses were still heated by wood-burning stoves.

Page 18

Analyze Text Structure
Reading: Literature

DIRECTIONS: Use the play to choose or write the best answer.

Strategy Use the parts of a story, play, or poem to help you identify the theme, setting, or plot. Look for the setting and plot events in the stage directions of a play. Look at the dialogue to find details about plot and theme.

Test Tip Compare the format of a play to a story to help you understand its parts. For example, a story has paragraphs, a play has scenes, and a poem has stanzas.

2. The stage directions describe the characters—who they are and, in some cases, how they feel. These clues suggest that people have come to the house to
   - ● investigate a crime
   - (B) get warm by the stove
   - (C) clean up the messy kitchen
   - (D) find out where the homeowners are

Write how you know.

Possible Answer: Two of the characters are in law enforcement, and the women are described as looking nervous and frightened. Something bad has happened, apparently, and the sheriff and county attorney must determine what.

3. Read lines 7 and 8 again. What does the long dash at the end of line 7 tell readers?
   - ● The attorney interrupts the sheriff.
   - (B) The sheriff has finished speaking.
   - (C) The sheriff notices that something was moved in the room.
   - (D) The attorney thinks the women have moved things in the room.

4. Reread lines 1 and 2, and look at the stage directions. What do the stage directions "after taking a step forward" and the sheriff's wife Mrs. Peters' reply suggest about her?
   - (A) For some reason, she is not cold like the others are.
   - (B) For some reason, she is not aware that the sheriff is being polite.
   - ● For some reason, she does not want to walk farther into the kitchen.
   - (D) For some reason, she does not like the sheriff or the county attorney.

5. Look at the dialogue markers in these lines. What do they suggest about which characters are in charge in the scene? Explain how you know.

Possible Answer: The county attorney and the sheriff are in charge. The dialogue markers show how they are the only people talking. The sheriff's wife says just three hesitant words. Mr. and Mrs. Hale never speak. The people who dominate the conversation are also in control of the scene.

Page 19

Explain the Narrator's Point of View
Reading: Literature

DIRECTIONS: Read the story. Then, answer the questions.

[1] A fox caught in a trap escaped but, in so doing, lost his tail. [2] Thereafter, feeling his life a burden from the shame and ridicule to which he was exposed, he schemed to convince the other foxes that being tailless was much more attractive, thus making up for his deprivation. [3] He assembled a good many foxes and publicly advised them to cut off their tails, saying they would not only look much better without them, but they would also get rid of the weight of the brush, which was a great inconvenience. [4] One of them, interrupting him, said, "If you had not, yourself, lost your tail, my friend, you would not thus counsel us."

Strategy Identify a narrator's point of view by reading story details carefully and looking for clues to who is telling the story. Then, think about how point of view affects the way the story is told.

Test Tip A first-person narrator knows only his or her own thoughts. Just as real people do, this narrator must infer other people's thoughts from what they do and say. When you read first-person point of view stories, ask, Is the narrator guessing other characters' thoughts correctly?

1. Part A: What point of view does the narrator use to tell the story of the fox and his tail?
   - (A) first person, as the fox himself
   - (B) third person, as the other foxes
   - ● third person, as someone outside the events
   - (D) first person, as the hunter who set the trap

Part B: Explain how you know.

Possible Answer: The narrator knows both how the fox feels after having lost his tail and what the other foxes think about his loss. The narrator refers to the characters as he and they. Only a third-person narrator tells the story in this way.

2. Which statement describes the narrator's attitude toward the fox?
   - (A) The narrator feels sorry for the fox because he lost his tail.
   - (B) The narrator agrees with the fox that it is better to do without a tail.
   - (C) The narrator thinks it was silly of the fox to let his tail get caught in the trap.
   - ● The narrator disapproves of the fox's trick to get other foxes to cut off their tails.

3. Explain how the story would be different if it were told in the opposite point of view.

Possible Answer: The fox would be the narrator if the story were told in first-person point of view. The fox would share what he was thinking and feeling about losing his tail. He might also share how he feels about what the one fox says to him.

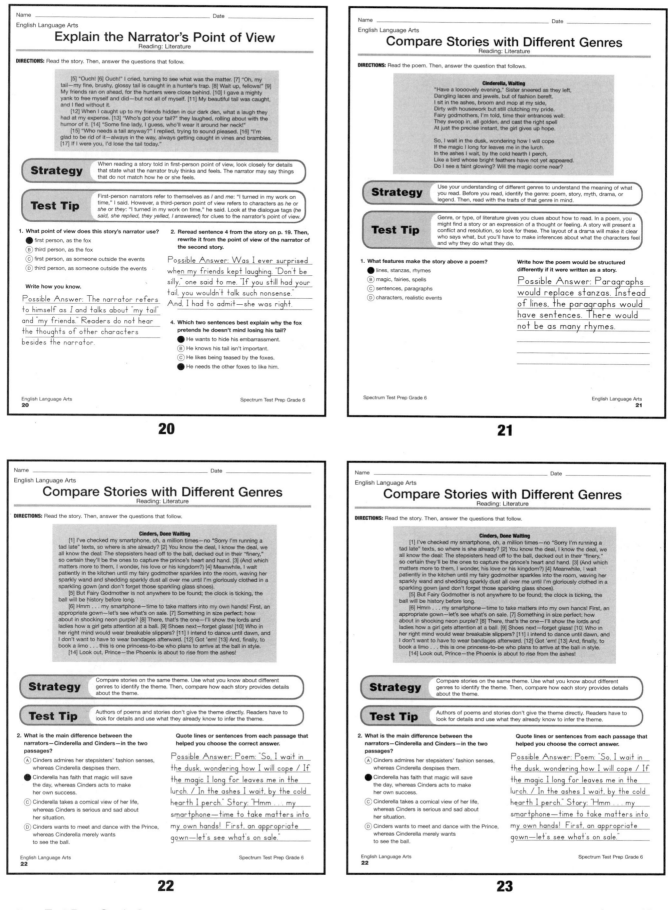

Page 20

Explain the Narrator's Point of View
Reading: Literature

DIRECTIONS: Read the story. Then, answer the questions that follow.

[5] "Ouch! [6] Ouch!" I cried, turning to see what was the matter. [7] "Oh, my tail—my fine, brushy, glossy tail is caught in a hunter's trap. [8] Wait up, fellows!" [9] My friends ran on ahead, for the hunters were close behind. [10] I gave a mighty yank to free myself and did—but not all of myself. [11] My beautiful tail was caught, and I fled without it.
[12] When I caught up to my friends hidden in our dark den, what a laugh they had at my expense. [13] "Who's got your tail?" they laughed, rolling about with the humor of it. [14] "Some fine lady, I guess, who'll wear it around her neck!"
[15] "Who needs a tail anyway!" I replied, trying to sound pleased. [16] "I'm glad to be rid of it—always in the way, always getting caught in vines and brambles. [17] If I were you, I'd lose the tail today."

Strategy — When reading a story told in first-person point of view, look closely for details that state what the narrator truly thinks and feels. The narrator may say things that do not match how he or she feels.

Test Tip — First-person narrators refer to themselves as *I* and *me*: "I turned in my work on time," I said. However, a third-person point of view refers to characters as *he* or *she* or *they*: "I turned in my work on time," he said. Look at the dialogue tags (*he said, she replied, they yelled, I answered*) for clues to the narrator's point of view.

1. What point of view does this story's narrator use?
   ● first person, as the fox
   Ⓑ third person, as the fox
   Ⓒ first person, as someone outside the events
   Ⓓ third person, as someone outside the events

Write how you know.

Possible Answer: The narrator refers to himself as *I* and talks about "my tail" and "my friends." Readers do not hear the thoughts of other characters besides the narrator.

2. Reread sentence 4 from the story on p. 19. Then, rewrite it from the point of view of the narrator of the second story.

Possible Answer: Was I ever surprised when my friends kept laughing. "Don't be silly," one said to me. "If you still had your tail, you wouldn't talk such nonsense." And, I had to admit—she was right.

4. Which two sentences best explain why the fox pretends he doesn't mind losing his tail?
   ● He wants to hide his embarrassment.
   Ⓑ He knows his tail isn't important.
   Ⓒ He likes being teased by the foxes.
   ● He needs the other foxes to like him.

Page 21

Compare Stories with Different Genres
Reading: Literature

DIRECTIONS: Read the poem. Then, answer the question that follows.

Cinderella, Waiting

"Have a loooovely evening," Sister sneered as they left,
Dangling laces and jewels, but of fashion bereft.
I sit in the ashes, broom and mop at my side,
Dirty with housework but still clutching my pride.
Fairy godmothers, I'm told, time their entrances well:
They swoop in, all golden, and cast the right spell
At just the precise instant, the girl gives up hope.

So, I wait in the dusk, wondering how I will cope
If the magic I long for leaves me in the lurch.
In the ashes I wait, by the cold hearth I perch,
Like a bird whose bright feathers have not yet appeared.
Do I see a faint glowing? Will the magic come near?

Strategy — Use your understanding of different genres to understand the meaning of what you read. Before you read, identify the genre: poem, story, myth, drama, or legend. Then, read with the traits of that genre in mind.

Test Tip — Genre, or type, of literature gives you clues about how to read. In a poem, you might find a story or an expression of a thought or feeling. A story will present a conflict and resolution, so look for these. The layout of a drama will make it clear who says what, but you'll have to make inferences about what the characters feel and why they do what they do.

1. What features make the story above a poem?
   ● lines, stanzas, rhymes
   Ⓑ magic, fairies, spells
   Ⓒ sentences, paragraphs
   Ⓓ characters, realistic events

Write how the poem would be structured differently if it were written as a story.

Possible Answer: Paragraphs would replace stanzas. Instead of lines, the paragraphs would have sentences. There would not be as many rhymes.

Page 22

Compare Stories with Different Genres
Reading: Literature

DIRECTIONS: Read the story. Then, answer the questions that follow.

Cinders, Done Waiting

[1] I've checked my smartphone, oh, a million times—no "Sorry I'm running a tad late" texts, so where is she already? [2] You know the deal, I know the deal, we all know the deal: The stepsisters head off to the ball, decked out in their "finery," so certain they'll be the ones to capture the prince's heart and hand. [3] (And which matters more to them, I wonder, his love or his kingdom?) [4] Meanwhile, I wait patiently in the kitchen until my fairy godmother sparkles into the room, waving her sparkly wand and shedding sparkly dust all over me until I'm gloriously clothed in a sparkling gown (and don't forget those sparkling glass shoes).
[5] But Fairy Godmother is not anywhere to be found; the clock is ticking, the ball will be history before long.
[6] Hmm . . . my smartphone—time to take matters into my own hands! First, an appropriate gown—let's see what's on sale. [7] Something in size perfect; how about in shocking neon purple? [8] There, that's the one—I'll show the lords and ladies how a girl gets attention at a ball. [9] Shoes next—forget glass! [10] Who in her right mind would wear breakable slippers? [11] I intend to dance until dawn, and I don't want to have to wear bandages afterward. [12] Got 'em! [13] And, finally, to book a limo . . . this is one princess-to-be who plans to arrive at the ball in style.
[14] Look out, Prince—the Phoenix is about to rise from the ashes!

Strategy — Compare stories on the same theme. Use what you know about different genres to identify the theme. Then, compare how each story provides details about the theme.

Test Tip — Authors of poems and stories don't give the theme directly. Readers have to look for details and use what they already know to infer the theme.

2. What is the main difference between the narrators—Cinderella and Cinders—in the two passages?
   Ⓐ Cinders admires her stepsisters' fashion senses, whereas Cinderella despises them.
   ● Cinderella has faith that magic will save the day, whereas Cinders acts to make her own success.
   Ⓒ Cinderella takes a comical view of her life, whereas Cinders is serious and sad about her situation.
   Ⓓ Cinders wants to meet and dance with the Prince, whereas Cinderella merely wants to see the ball.

Quote lines or sentences from each passage that helped you choose the correct answer.

Possible Answer: Poem: "So, I wait in the dusk, wondering how I will cope / If the magic I long for leaves me in the lurch. / In the ashes I wait, by the cold hearth I perch." Story: "Hmm . . . my smartphone—time to take matters into my own hands! First, an appropriate gown—let's see what's on sale."

Page 23

Compare Stories with Different Genres
Reading: Literature

DIRECTIONS: Read the story. Then, answer the questions that follow.

Cinders, Done Waiting

[1] I've checked my smartphone, oh, a million times—no "Sorry I'm running a tad late" texts, so where is she already? [2] You know the deal, I know the deal, we all know the deal: The stepsisters head off to the ball, decked out in their "finery," so certain they'll be the ones to capture the prince's heart and hand. [3] (And which matters more to them, I wonder, his love or his kingdom?) [4] Meanwhile, i wait patiently in the kitchen until my fairy godmother sparkles into the room, waving her sparkly wand and shedding sparkly dust all over me until I'm gloriously clothed in a sparkling gown (and don't forget those sparkling glass shoes).
[5] But Fairy Godmother is not anywhere to be found; the clock is ticking, the ball will be history before long.
[6] Hmm . . . my smartphone—time to take matters into my own hands! First, an appropriate gown—let's see what's on sale. [7] Something in size perfect; how about in shocking neon purple? [8] There, that's the one—I'll show the lords and ladies how a girl gets attention at a ball. [9] Shoes next—forget glass! [10] Who in her right mind would wear breakable slippers? [11] I intend to dance until dawn, and I don't want to have to wear bandages afterward. [12] Got 'em! [13] And, finally, to book a limo . . . this is one princess-to-be who plans to arrive at the ball in style.
[14] Look out, Prince—the Phoenix is about to rise from the ashes!

Strategy — Compare stories on the same theme. Use what you know about different genres to identify the theme. Then, compare how each story provides details about the theme.

Test Tip — Authors of poems and stories don't give the theme directly. Readers have to look for details and use what they already know to infer the theme.

2. What is the main difference between the narrators—Cinderella and Cinders—in the two passages?
   Ⓐ Cinders admires her stepsisters' fashion senses, whereas Cinderella despises them.
   ● Cinderella has faith that magic will save the day, whereas Cinders acts to make her own success.
   Ⓒ Cinderella takes a comical view of her life, whereas Cinders is serious and sad about her situation.
   Ⓓ Cinders wants to meet and dance with the Prince, whereas Cinderella merely wants to see the ball.

Quote lines or sentences from each passage that helped you choose the correct answer.

Possible Answer: Poem: "So, I wait in the dusk, wondering how I will cope / If the magic I long for leaves me in the lurch. / In the ashes I wait, by the cold hearth I perch." Story: "Hmm . . . my smartphone—time to take matters into my own hands! First, an appropriate gown—let's see what's on sale."

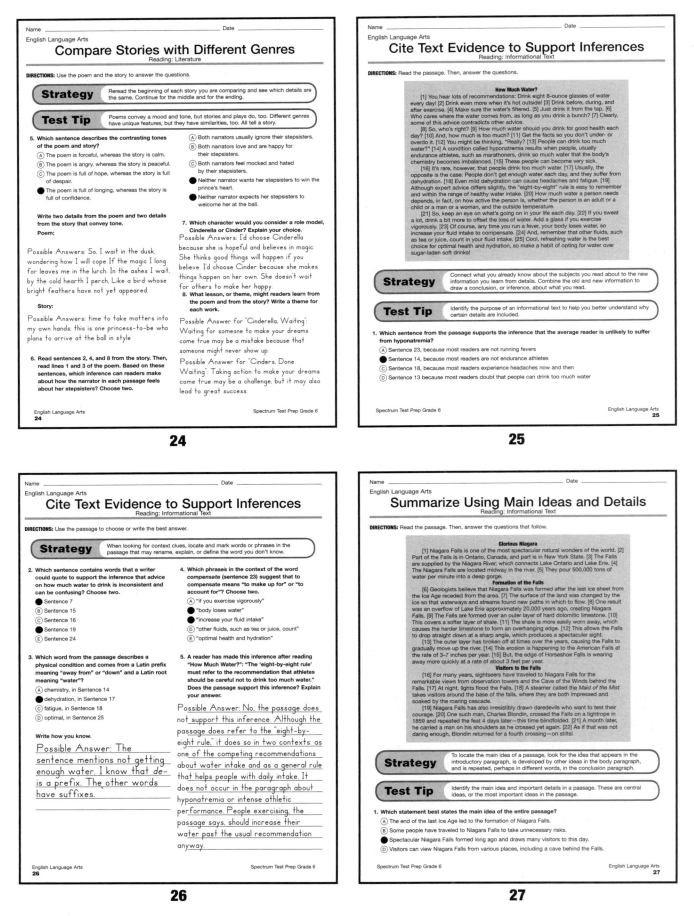

Page 24

Compare Stories with Different Genres
Reading: Literature

DIRECTIONS: Use the poem and the story to answer the questions.

Strategy Reread the beginning of each story you are comparing and see which details are the same. Continue for the middle and for the ending.

Test Tip Poems convey a mood and tone, but stories and plays do, too. Different genres have unique features, but they have similarities, too. All tell a story.

5. Which sentence describes the contrasting tones of the poem and story?

(A) The poem is forceful, whereas the story is calm.

(B) The poem is angry, whereas the story is peaceful.

(C) The poem is full of hope, whereas the story is full of despair.

● The poem is full of longing, whereas the story is full of confidence.

Write two details from the poem and two details from the story that convey tone.

Poem:

Possible Answers: So, I wait in the dusk, wondering how I will cope If the magic I long for leaves me in the lurch. In the ashes I wait, by the cold hearth I perch. Like a bird whose bright feathers have not yet appeared.

Story:

Possible Answers: time to take matters into my own hands; this is one princess-to-be who plans to arrive at the ball in style

6. Read sentences 2, 4, and 8 from the story. Then, read lines 1 and 3 of the poem. Based on these sentences, which inference can readers make about how the narrator in each passage feels about her stepsisters? Choose two.

(A) Both narrators usually ignore their stepsisters.

(B) Both narrators love and are happy for their stepsisters.

(C) Both narrators feel mocked and hated by their stepsisters.

● Neither narrator wants her stepsisters to win the prince's heart.

● Neither narrator expects her stepsisters to welcome her at the ball.

7. Which character would you consider a role model, Cinderella or Cinder? Explain your choice.

Possible Answers: I'd choose Cinderella because she is hopeful and believes in magic. She thinks good things will happen if you believe. I'd choose Cinder because she makes things happen on her own. She doesn't wait for others to make her happy.

8. What lesson, or theme, might readers learn from the poem and from the story? Write a theme for each work.

Possible Answer for "Cinderella, Waiting": Waiting for someone to make your dreams come true may be a mistake because that someone might never show up.

Possible Answer for "Cinders, Done Waiting": Taking action to make your dreams come true may be a challenge, but it may also lead to great success.

24

Page 25

Cite Text Evidence to Support Inferences
Reading: Informational Text

DIRECTIONS: Read the passage. Then, answer the questions.

How Much Water?

[1] You hear lots of recommendations: Drink eight 8-ounce glasses of water every day! [2] Drink even more when it's hot outside! [3] Drink before, during, and after exercise. [4] Make sure the water's filtered. [5] Just drink it from the tap. [6] Who cares where the water comes from, as long as you drink a bunch? [7] Clearly, some of this advice contradicts other advice.

[8] So, who's right? [9] How much water should you drink for good health each day? [10] And, how much is too much? [11] Get the facts so you don't under- or overdo it. [12] You might be thinking, "Really? [13] People can drink too much water?" [14] A condition called hyponatremia results when people, usually endurance athletes, such as marathoners, drink so much water that the body's chemistry becomes imbalanced. [15] These people can become very sick.

[16] It's rare, however, that people drink too much water. [17] Usually, the opposite is the case: People don't get enough water each day, and they suffer from dehydration. [18] Even mild dehydration can cause headaches and fatigue. [19] Although expert advice differs slightly, the "eight-by-eight" rule is easy to remember and within the range of healthy water intake. [20] How much water a person needs depends, in fact, on how active the person is, whether the person is an adult or a child or a man or a woman, and the outside temperature.

[21] So, keep an eye on what's going on in your life each day. [22] If you sweat a lot, drink a bit more to offset the loss of water. [23] Of course, any time you run a fever, your body loses water, so increase your fluid intake to compensate. [24] And, remember that other fluids, such as tea or juice, count in your fluid intake. [25] Cool, refreshing water is the best choice for optimal health and hydration, so make a habit of opting for water over sugar-laden soft drinks!

Strategy Connect what you already know about the subjects you read about to the new information you learn from details. Combine the old and new information to draw a conclusion, or inference, about what you read.

Test Tip Identify the purpose of an informational text to help you better understand why certain details are included.

1. Which sentence from the passage supports the inference that the average reader is unlikely to suffer from hyponatremia?

(A) Sentence 23, because most readers are not running fevers

● Sentence 14, because most readers are not endurance athletes

(C) Sentence 18, because most readers experience headaches now and then

(D) Sentence 13 because most readers doubt that people can drink too much water

25

Page 26

Cite Text Evidence to Support Inferences
Reading: Informational Text

DIRECTIONS: Use the passage to choose or write the best answer.

Strategy When looking for context clues, locate and mark words or phrases in the passage that may rename, explain, or define the word you don't know.

2. Which sentence contains words that a writer could quote to support the inference that advice on how much water to drink is inconsistent and can be confusing? Choose two.

● Sentence 7

(B) Sentence 15

(C) Sentence 16

(D) Sentence 19

(E) Sentence 24

3. Which word from the passage describes a physical condition and comes from a Latin prefix meaning "away from" or "down" and a Latin root meaning "water"?

(A) chemistry, in Sentence 14

● dehydration, in Sentence 17

(C) fatigue, in Sentence 18

(D) optimal, in Sentence 25

Write how you know.

Possible Answer: The sentence mentions not getting enough water. I know that de- is a prefix. The other words have suffixes.

4. Which phrases in the context of the word *compensate* (sentence 23) suggest that to compensate means "to make up for" or "to account for"? Choose two.

(A) "if you exercise vigorously"

● "body loses water"

● "increase your fluid intake"

(D) "other fluids, such as tea or juice, count"

(E) "optimal health and hydration"

5. A reader has made this inference after reading "How Much Water?": The 'eight-by-eight rule' must refer to the recommendation that athletes should be careful not to drink too much water." Does the passage support this inference? Explain your answer.

Possible Answer: No, the passage does not support this inference. Although the passage does refer to the "eight-by-eight rule," it does so in two contexts: as one of the competing recommendations about water intake and as a general rule that helps people with daily intake. It does not occur in the paragraph about hyponatremia or intense athletic performance. People exercising, the passage says, should increase their water past the usual recommendation anyway.

26

Page 27

Summarize Using Main Ideas and Details
Reading: Informational Text

DIRECTIONS: Read the passage. Then, answer the questions that follow.

Glorious Niagara

[1] Niagara Falls is one of the most spectacular natural wonders of the world. [2] Part of the Falls is in Ontario, Canada, and part is in New York State. [3] The Falls are supplied by the Niagara River, which connects Lake Ontario and Lake Erie. [4] The Niagara Falls are located midway in the river. [5] They pour 500,000 tons of water per minute into a deep gorge.

Formation of the Falls

[6] Geologists believe that Niagara Falls was formed after the last ice sheet from the Ice Age receded from the area. [7] The surface of the land was changed by the ice so that waterways and streams found new paths in which to flow. [8] One result was an overflow of Lake Erie approximately 20,000 years ago, creating Niagara Falls. [9] The Falls are formed over an outer layer of hard dolomitic limestone. [10] This covers a softer layer of shale. [11] The shale is more easily worn away, which causes the harder limestone to form an overhanging edge. [12] This allows the Falls to drop straight down at a sharp angle, which produces a spectacular sight. [13] The outer layer has broken off at times over the years, causing the Falls to gradually move up the river. [14] This erosion is happening to the American Falls at the rate of 3–7 inches per year. [15] But, the edge of Horseshoe Falls is wearing away more quickly at a rate of about 3 feet per year.

Visitors to the Falls

[16] For many years, sightseers have traveled to Niagara Falls for the remarkable views from observation towers and the Cave of the Winds behind the Falls. [17] At night, lights flood the Falls. [18] A steamer called the *Maid of the Mist* takes visitors around the base of the falls, where they are both impressed and soaked by the roaring cascade.

[19] Niagara Falls has also irresistibly drawn daredevils who want to test their courage. [20] One such man, Charles Blondin, crossed the Falls on a tightrope in 1859 and repeated the feat 4 days later—this time blindfolded. [21] A month later, he carried a man on his shoulders as he crossed yet again. [22] As if that wasn't daring enough, Blondin returned for a fourth crossing—on stilts!

Strategy To locate the main idea of a passage, look for the idea that appears in the introductory paragraph, is developed by other ideas in the body paragraph, and is repeated, perhaps in different words, in the conclusion paragraph.

Test Tip Identify the main idea and important details in a passage. These are central ideas, or the most important ideas in the passage.

1. Which statement best states the main idea of the entire passage?

(A) The end of the last Ice Age led to the formation of Niagara Falls.

(B) Some people have traveled to Niagara Falls to take unnecessary risks.

● Spectacular Niagara Falls formed long ago and draws many visitors to this day.

(D) Visitors can view Niagara Falls from various places, including a cave behind the Falls.

27

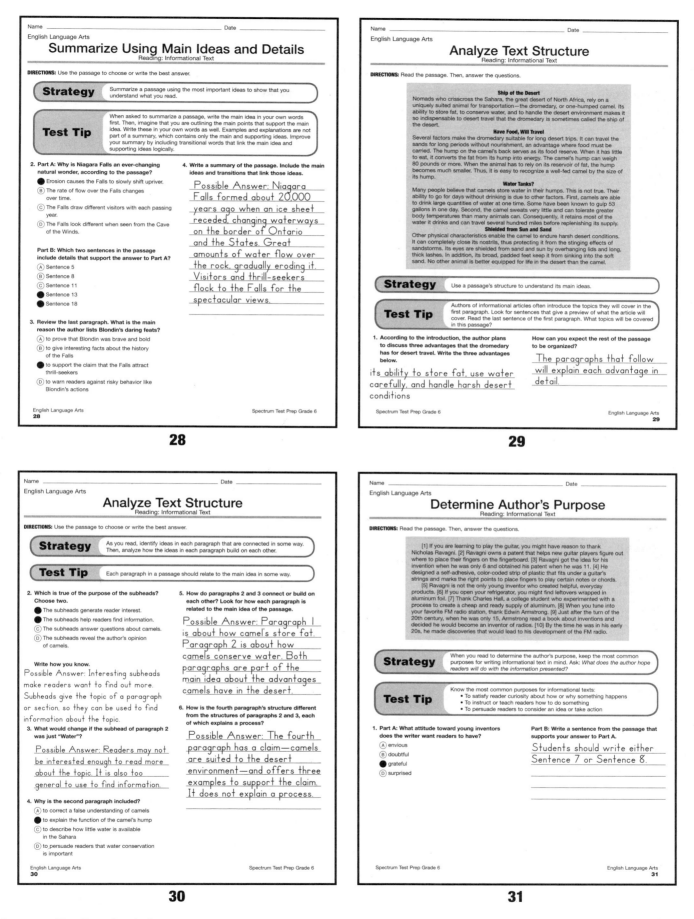

Summarize Using Main Ideas and Details
Reading: Informational Text

DIRECTIONS: Use the passage to choose or write the best answer.

Strategy Summarize a passage using the most important ideas to show that you understand what you read.

Test Tip When asked to summarize a passage, write the main idea in your own words first. Then, imagine that you are outlining the main points that support the main idea. Write these in your own words as well. Examples and explanations are not part of a summary, which contains only the main and supporting ideas. Improve your summary by including transitional words that link the main idea and supporting ideas logically.

2. **Part A: Why is Niagara Falls an ever-changing natural wonder, according to the passage?**
● A Erosion causes the Falls to slowly shift upriver.
○ B The rate of flow over the Falls changes over time.
○ C The Falls draw different visitors with each passing year.
○ D The Falls look different when seen from the Cave of the Winds.

Part B: Which two sentences in the passage include details that support the answer to Part A?
○ A Sentence 5
○ B Sentence 8
○ C Sentence 11
● Sentence 13
● Sentence 18

3. **Review the last paragraph. What is the main reason the author lists Blondin's daring feats?**
○ A to prove that Blondin was brave and bold
○ B to give interesting facts about the history of the Falls
● to support the claim that the Falls attract thrill-seekers
○ D to warn readers against risky behavior like Blondin's actions

4. **Write a summary of the passage. Include the main ideas and transitions that link those ideas.**

Possible Answer: Niagara Falls formed about 20,000 years ago when an ice sheet receded, changing waterways on the border of Ontario and the States. Great amounts of water flow over the rock, gradually eroding it. Visitors and thrill-seekers flock to the Falls for the spectacular views.

Analyze Text Structure
Reading: Informational Text

DIRECTIONS: Read the passage. Then, answer the questions.

Ship of the Desert
Nomads who crisscross the Sahara, the great desert of North Africa, rely on a uniquely suited animal for transportation—the dromedary, or one-humped camel. Its ability to store fat, to conserve water, and to handle the desert environment makes it so indispensable to desert travel that the dromedary is sometimes called the ship of the desert.

Have Food, Will Travel
Several factors make the dromedary suitable for long desert trips. It can travel the sands for long periods without nourishment, an advantage where food must be carried. The hump on the camel's back provides its food reserve. When it has little to eat, it converts the fat from its hump into energy. The camel's hump can weigh 80 pounds or more. When the animal has used up its reservoir of fat, the hump becomes much smaller. Thus, it is easy to recognize a well-fed camel by the size of its hump.

Water Tanks?
Many people believe that camels store water in their humps. This is not true. Their ability to go for days without drinking is due to other factors. First, camels are able to drink large quantities of water at one time. Some have been known to gulp 53 gallons in one day. Second, the camel sweats very little and can tolerate greater body temperatures than many animals can. Consequently, it retains most of the water it drinks and can travel several hundred miles before replenishing its supply.

Shielded from Sun and Sand
Other physical characteristics enable the camel to endure harsh desert conditions. It can completely close its nostrils, thus protecting it from the stinging effects of sandstorms. Its eyes are shielded from sand and sun by overhanging lids and long, thick lashes. In addition, its broad, padded feet keep it from sinking into the soft sand. No other animal is better equipped for life in the desert than the camel.

Strategy Use a passage's structure to understand its main ideas.

Test Tip Authors of informational articles often introduce the topics they will cover in the first paragraph. Look for sentences that give a preview of what the article will cover. Read the last sentence of the first paragraph. What topics will be covered in this passage?

1. According to the introduction, the author plans to discuss three advantages that the dromedary has for desert travel. Write the three advantages below.

its ability to store fat, use water carefully, and handle harsh desert conditions

How can you expect the rest of the passage to be organized?

The paragraphs that follow will explain each advantage in detail.

Analyze Text Structure
Reading: Informational Text

DIRECTIONS: Use the passage to choose or write the best answer.

Strategy As you read, identify ideas in each paragraph that are connected in some way. Then, analyze how the ideas in each paragraph build on each other.

Test Tip Each paragraph in a passage should relate to the main idea in some way.

2. **Which is true of the purpose of the subheads? Choose two.**
● The subheads generate reader interest.
● The subheads help readers find information.
○ C The subheads answer questions about camels.
○ D The subheads reveal the author's opinion of camels.

Write how you know.
Possible Answer: Interesting subheads make readers want to find out more. Subheads give the topic of a paragraph or section, so they can be used to find information about the topic.

3. **What would change if the subhead of paragraph 2 was just "Water"?**
Possible Answer: Readers may not be interested enough to read more about the topic. It is also too general to use to find information.

4. **Why is the second paragraph included?**
○ A to correct a false understanding of camels
● to explain the function of the camel's hump
○ C to describe how little water is available in the Sahara
○ D to persuade readers that water conservation is important

5. **How do paragraphs 2 and 3 connect or build on each other? Look for how each paragraph is related to the main idea of the passage.**
Possible Answer: Paragraph 1 is about how camel's store fat. Paragraph 2 is about how camels conserve water. Both paragraphs are part of the main idea about the advantages camels have in the desert.

6. **How is the fourth paragraph's structure different from the structures of paragraphs 2 and 3, each of which explains a process?**
Possible Answer: The fourth paragraph has a claim—camels are suited to the desert environment—and offers three examples to support the claim. It does not explain a process.

Determine Author's Purpose
Reading: Informational Text

DIRECTIONS: Read the passage. Then, answer the questions.

[1] If you are learning to play the guitar, you might have reason to thank Nicholas Ravagni. [2] Ravagni owns a patent that helps new guitar players figure out where to place their fingers on the fingerboard. [3] Ravagni got the idea for his invention when he was only 6 and obtained his patent when he was 11. [4] He designed a self-adhesive, color-coded strip of plastic that fits under a guitar's strings and marks the right points to place fingers to play certain notes or chords.
[5] Ravagni is not the only inventor who created helpful, everyday products. [6] If you open your refrigerator, you might find leftovers wrapped in aluminum foil. [7] Thank Charles Hall, a college student who experimented with a process to create a cheap and ready supply of aluminum. [8] When you tune into your favorite FM radio station, thank Edwin Armstrong. [9] Just after the turn of the 20th century, when he was only 15, Armstrong read a book about inventions and decided he would become an inventor of radios. [10] By the time he was in his early 20s, he made discoveries that would lead to his development of the FM radio.

Strategy When you read to determine the author's purpose, keep the most common purposes for writing informational text in mind. Ask: *What does the author hope readers will do with the information presented?*

Test Tip Know the most common purposes for informational texts:
• To satisfy reader curiosity about how or why something happens
• To instruct or teach readers how to do something
• To persuade readers to consider an idea or take action

1. **Part A: What attitude toward young inventors does the writer want readers to have?**
○ A envious
○ B doubtful
● grateful
○ D surprised

Part B: Write a sentence from the passage that supports your answer to Part A.
Students should write either Sentence 7 or Sentence 8.

Determine Author's Purpose
Reading: Informational Text

DIRECTIONS: Use the passage to choose or write the best answer.

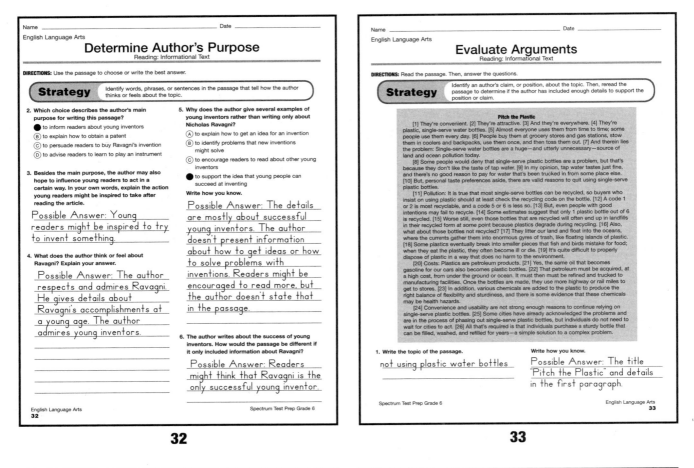

Strategy Identify words, phrases, or sentences in the passage that tell how the author thinks or feels about the topic.

2. Which choice describes the author's main purpose for writing this passage?
● (A) to inform readers about young inventors
(B) to explain how to obtain a patent
(C) to persuade readers to buy Ravagni's invention
(D) to advise readers to learn to play an instrument

3. Besides the main purpose, the author may also hope to influence young readers to act in a certain way. In your own words, explain the action young readers might be inspired to take after reading the article.

Possible Answer: Young readers might be inspired to try to invent something.

4. What does the author think or feel about Ravagni? Explain your answer.

Possible Answer: The author respects and admires Ravagni. He gives details about Ravagni's accomplishments at a young age. The author admires young inventors.

5. Why does the author give several examples of young inventors rather than writing only about Nicholas Ravagni?
(A) to explain how to get an idea for an invention
(B) to identify problems that new inventions might solve
(C) to encourage readers to read about other young inventors
● to support the idea that young people can succeed at inventing

Write how you know.

Possible Answer: The details are mostly about successful young inventors. The author doesn't present information about how to get ideas or how to solve problems with inventions. Readers might be encouraged to read more, but the author doesn't state that in the passage.

6. The author writes about the success of young inventors. How would the passage be different if it only included information about Ravagni?

Possible Answer: Readers might think that Ravagni is the only successful young inventor.

32

Evaluate Arguments
Reading: Informational Text

DIRECTIONS: Read the passage. Then, answer the questions.

Strategy Identify an author's claim, or position, about the topic. Then, reread the passage to determine if the author has included enough details to support the position or claim.

Pitch the Plastic

[1] They're convenient. [2] They're attractive. [3] And they're everywhere. [4] They're plastic, single-serve water bottles. [5] Almost everyone uses them from time to time; some people use them every day. [6] People buy them at grocery stores and gas stations, stow them in coolers and backpacks, use them once, and then toss them out. [7] And therein lies the problem: Single-serve water bottles are a huge—and utterly unnecessary—source of land and ocean pollution today.

[8] Some people would deny that single-serve plastic bottles are a problem, but that's because they don't like the taste of tap water. [9] In my opinion, tap water tastes just fine, and there's no good reason to pay for water that's been trucked in from some place else. [10] But, personal taste preferences aside, there are valid reasons to quit using single-serve plastic bottles.

[11] Pollution: It is true that most single-serve bottles can be recycled, so buyers who insist on using plastic should at least check the recycling code on the bottle. [12] A code 1 or 2 is most recyclable, and a code 5 or 6 is less so. [13] But, even people with good intentions may fail to recycle. [14] Some estimates suggest that only 1 plastic bottle out of 6 is recycled. [15] Worse still, even those bottles that are recycled will often end up in landfills in their recycled form at some point because plastics degrade during recycling. [16] Also, what about those bottles not recycled? [17] They litter our land and float into the oceans, where the currents gather them into enormous gyres of trash, like floating islands of plastic. [18] Some plastics eventually break into smaller pieces that fish and birds mistake for food; when they eat the plastic, they often become ill or die. [19] It's quite difficult to properly dispose of plastic in a way that does no harm to the environment.

[20] Costs: Plastics are petroleum products. [21] Yes, the same oil that becomes gasoline for our cars also becomes plastic bottles. [22] That petroleum must be acquired, at a high cost, from under the ground or ocean. It must then must be refined and trucked to manufacturing facilities. Once the bottles are made, they use more highway or rail miles to get to stores. [23] In addition, various chemicals are added to the plastic to produce the right balance of flexibility and sturdiness, and there is some evidence that these chemicals may be health hazards.

[24] Convenience and usability are not strong enough reasons to continue relying on single-serve plastic bottles. [25] Some cities have already acknowledged the problems and are in the process of phasing out single-serve plastic bottles, but individuals do not need to wait for cities to act. [26] All that's required is that individuals purchase a sturdy bottle that can be filled, washed, and refilled for years—a simple solution to a complex problem.

1. Write the topic of the passage.

not using plastic water bottles

Write how you know.

Possible Answer: The title "Pitch the Plastic" and details in the first paragraph.

33

Evaluate Arguments
Reading: Informational Text

DIRECTIONS: Use the passage to choose or write the best answer.

Test Tip A claim is an opinion or idea that an author has about a topic. A position is the side the author takes on a controversial issue.

2. What technique does the author use to introduce the topic in the first paragraph? Choose three.
(A) She describes the pollution caused by plastic bottles.
● She grabs the reader's attention with short, parallel sentences.
● She creates suspense, not telling the reader until Sentence 4 to find out what "they" are.
(D) She appeals to the reader's desire to save money and help the environment.
● She presents what sounds like a good thing and then suddenly announces it is a bad thing.

3. Part A: Which statement accurately summarizes the author's claim about why so many people use single-serve plastic bottles?
(A) People intend to recycle all the bottles they use.
(B) People are not aware of the real cost of these bottles.
(C) People do not mind paying extra to have water in these bottles.
● People think the water in these bottles tastes better than tap water.

Part B: What type of evidence is used to support this claim?
● the author's personal tastes
(B) scientific research into water quality
(C) taste tests of bottled water and tap water
(D) industry research on the market for bottled water

Part C: Why is the author's explanation in the second paragraph about why people choose single-serve plastic bottles an example of a weak argument and evidence?

Possible Answer: The author gives no sources for her claims; she simply assumes the reason people buy the bottles and then adds her own opinion. That means she misses the real reasons people use these bottles and passes up opportunities to counter these reasons.

34

Evaluate Arguments
Reading: Informational Text

DIRECTIONS: Use the passage to choose or write the best answer.

Strategy Mark the passage as you read, looking for evidence to support the claim. Use question marks to mark evidence you find doubtful, and use stars to mark evidence you find convincing.

4. What evidence does the author give that recycling is not an adequate solution to the plastic-bottle problem? Choose two.
● Most plastic bottles are simply thrown away.
(B) Some cities have decided to ban plastic bottles.
(B) Bits of plastic bottles can kill fish and sea birds.
● Plastic degrades when it is made into something else.

Test Tip

Check the credibility of an author's sources by thinking about who did the research the author cites. Were the researchers unbiased, seeking only the facts and not thinking about how the research might help them make money? Or, were they looking for information to support their own position? Unbiased research is more credible than research done to support a position or help a business make more money.

5. The author checked several sources to get information about the costs of plastic production. Read the information about each source. For each source, write "likely unbiased, more credible" or "possibly biased, less credible" on the line.

First source: a report on petroleum costs written by a major oil producer and refiner

possibly biased, less credible

Second source: a government-funded study of costs to repair highways and rail lines used to move manufactured goods to stores

likely unbiased, more credible

Third source: an interview with the manager of a factory where reusable metal bottles are made

possibly biased, less credible

6. Which of the three sources in question 5 is the least credible? Explain your reasoning.

Possible Answer: Students should explain that the report in the first source or the interview in the third source may be biased because the oil company and factory manager stand to earn money if the research supports their business.

7. If you wanted to find additional evidence to support the claim that plastic bottles are a major source of ocean pollution, which source would likely provide unbiased, credible evidence? Choose two.
(A) a blog on ocean travel written by a world traveler
● photographs and maps showing plastic islands in the oceans
(C) personal stories of a friend who cleans up plastic trash along the shoreline
● an article by a wildlife biologist who has found plastic bits in dead sea birds' stomachs

35

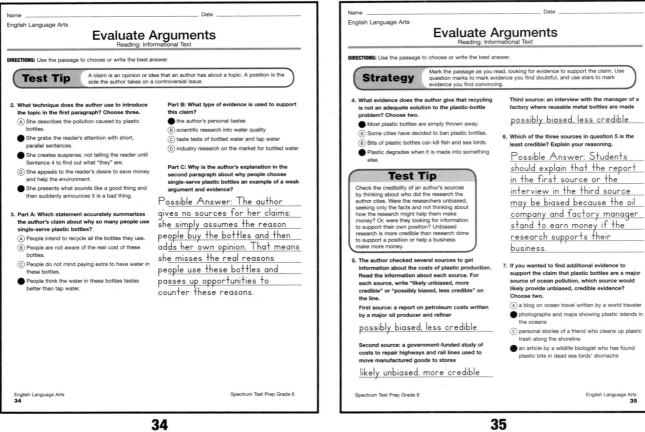

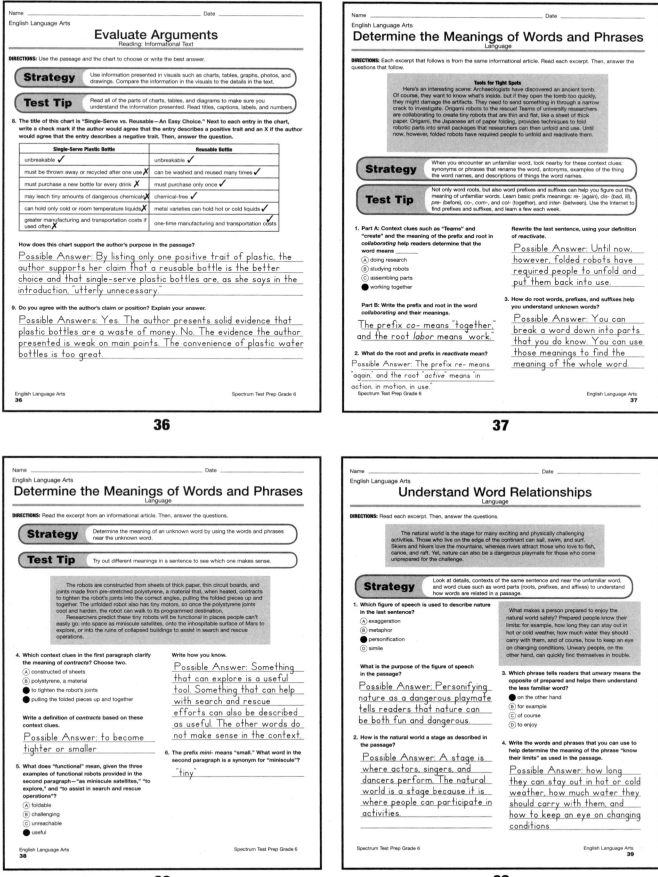

Page 36

Evaluate Arguments
Reading: Informational Text

DIRECTIONS: Use the passage and the chart to choose or write the best answer.

Strategy Use information presented in visuals such as charts, tables, graphs, photos, and drawings. Compare the information in the visuals to the details in the text.

Test Tip Read all of the parts of charts, tables, and diagrams to make sure you understand the information presented. Read titles, captions, labels, and numbers.

8. The title of this chart is "Single-Serve vs. Reusable—An Easy Choice." Next to each entry in the chart, write a check mark if the author would agree that the entry describes a positive trait and an X if the author would agree that the entry describes a negative trait. Then, answer the question.

Single-Serve Plastic Bottle	Reusable Bottle
unbreakable ✓	unbreakable ✓
must be thrown away or recycled after one use ✗	can be washed and reused many times ✓
must purchase a new bottle for every drink ✗	must purchase only once ✓
may leach tiny amounts of dangerous chemicals ✗	chemical-free ✓
can hold only cold or room temperature liquids ✗	metal varieties can hold hot or cold liquids ✓
greater manufacturing and transportation costs if used often ✗	one-time manufacturing and transportation costs ✓

How does this chart support the author's purpose in the passage?

Possible Answer: By listing only one positive trait of plastic, the author supports her claim that a reusable bottle is the better choice and that single-serve plastic bottles are, as she says in the introduction, "utterly unnecessary."

9. Do you agree with the author's claim or position? Explain your answer.

Possible Answers: Yes. The author presents solid evidence that plastic bottles are a waste of money. No. The evidence the author presented is weak on main points. The convenience of plastic water bottles is too great.

36

Page 37

Determine the Meanings of Words and Phrases
Language

DIRECTIONS: Each excerpt that follows is from the same informational article. Read each excerpt. Then, answer the questions that follow.

Tools for Tight Spots

Here's an interesting scene: Archaeologists have discovered an ancient tomb. Of course, they want to know what's inside, but if they open the tomb too quickly, they might damage the artifacts. They need to send something in through a narrow crack to investigate. Origami robots to the rescue! Teams of university researchers are collaborating to create tiny robots that are thin and flat, like a sheet of thick paper. Origami, the Japanese art of paper folding, provides techniques to fold robotic parts into small packages that researchers can then unfold and use. Until now, however, folded robots have required people to unfold and reactivate them.

Strategy When you encounter an unfamiliar word, look nearby for these context clues: synonyms or phrases that rename the word, antonyms, examples of the thing the word names, and descriptions of things the word names.

Test Tip Not only word roots, but also word prefixes and suffixes can help you figure out the meaning of unfamiliar words. Learn basic prefix meanings: re- (again), dis- (bad, ill), pre- (before), co-, com-, and col- (together), and inter- (between). Use the Internet to find prefixes and suffixes, and learn a few each week.

1. **Part A:** Context clues such as "Teams" and "create" and the meaning of the prefix and root in *collaborating* help readers determine that the word means _____
   Ⓐ doing research
   Ⓑ studying robots
   Ⓒ assembling parts
   ● working together

   Part B: Write the prefix and root in the word *collaborating* and their meanings.

   The prefix co- means "together," and the root labor means "work."

2. What do the root and prefix in *reactivate* mean?
   Possible Answer: The prefix re- means "again," and the root active means "in action, in motion, in use."

Rewrite the last sentence, using your definition of *reactivate*.

Possible Answer: Until now, however, folded robots have required people to unfold and put them back into use.

3. How do root words, prefixes, and suffixes help you understand unknown words?

Possible Answer: You can break a word down into parts that you do know. You can use those meanings to find the meaning of the whole word.

37

Page 38

Determine the Meanings of Words and Phrases
Language

DIRECTIONS: Read the excerpt from an informational article. Then, answer the questions.

Strategy Determine the meaning of an unknown word by using the words and phrases near the unknown word.

Test Tip Try out different meanings in a sentence to see which one makes sense.

The robots are constructed from sheets of thick paper, thin circuit boards, and joints made from pre-stretched polystyrene, a material that, when heated, contracts to tighten the robot's joints into the correct angles, pulling the folded pieces up and together. The unfolded robot also has tiny motors, so once the polystyrene joints cool and harden, the robot can walk to its programmed destination.

Researchers predict these tiny robots will be functional in places people can't easily go: into space as miniscule satellites, onto the inhospitable surface of Mars to explore, or into the ruins of collapsed buildings to assist in search and rescue operations.

4. Which context clues in the first paragraph clarify the meaning of *contracts*? Choose two.
   Ⓐ constructed of sheets
   Ⓑ polystyrene, a material
   ● to tighten the robot's joints
   ● pulling the folded pieces up and together

   Write a definition of *contracts* based on these context clues.

   Possible Answer: to become tighter or smaller

5. What does "functional" mean, given the three examples of functional robots provided in the second paragraph—"as miniscule satellites," "to explore," and "to assist in search and rescue operations"?
   Ⓐ foldable
   Ⓑ challenging
   Ⓒ unreachable
   ● useful

Write how you know.

Possible Answer: Something that can explore is a useful tool. Something that can help with search and rescue efforts can also be described as useful. The other words do not make sense in the context.

6. The prefix *mini-* means "small." What word in the second paragraph is a synonym for "miniscule"?

"tiny"

38

Page 39

Understand Word Relationships
Language

DIRECTIONS: Read each excerpt. Then, answer the questions.

The natural world is the stage for many exciting and physically challenging activities. Those who live on the edge of the continent can sail, swim, and surf. Skiers and hikers love the mountains, whereas rivers attract those who love to fish, canoe, and raft. Yet, nature can also be a dangerous playmate for those who come unprepared for the challenge.

Strategy Look at details, contexts of the same sentence and near the unfamiliar word, and word clues such as word parts (roots, prefixes, and affixes) to understand how words are related in a passage.

1. Which figure of speech is used to describe nature in the last sentence?
   Ⓐ exaggeration
   Ⓑ metaphor
   ● personification
   Ⓓ simile

   What is the purpose of the figure of speech in the passage?

   Possible Answer: Personifying nature as a dangerous playmate tells readers that nature can be both fun and dangerous.

2. How is the natural world a stage as described in the passage?

   Possible Answer: A stage is where actors, singers, and dancers perform. The natural world is a stage because it is where people can participate in activities.

What makes a person prepared to enjoy the natural world safely? Prepared people know their limits: for example, how long they can stay out in hot or cold weather, how much water they should carry with them, and of course, how to keep an eye on changing conditions. Unwary people, on the other hand, can quickly find themselves in trouble.

3. Which phrase tells readers that *unwary* means the opposite of prepared and helps them understand the less familiar word?
   ● on the other hand
   Ⓑ for example
   Ⓒ of course
   Ⓓ to enjoy

4. Write the words and phrases that you can use to help determine the meaning of the phrase "know their limits" as used in the passage.

   Possible Answer: how long they can stay out in hot or cold weather, how much water they should carry with them, and how to keep an eye on changing conditions

39

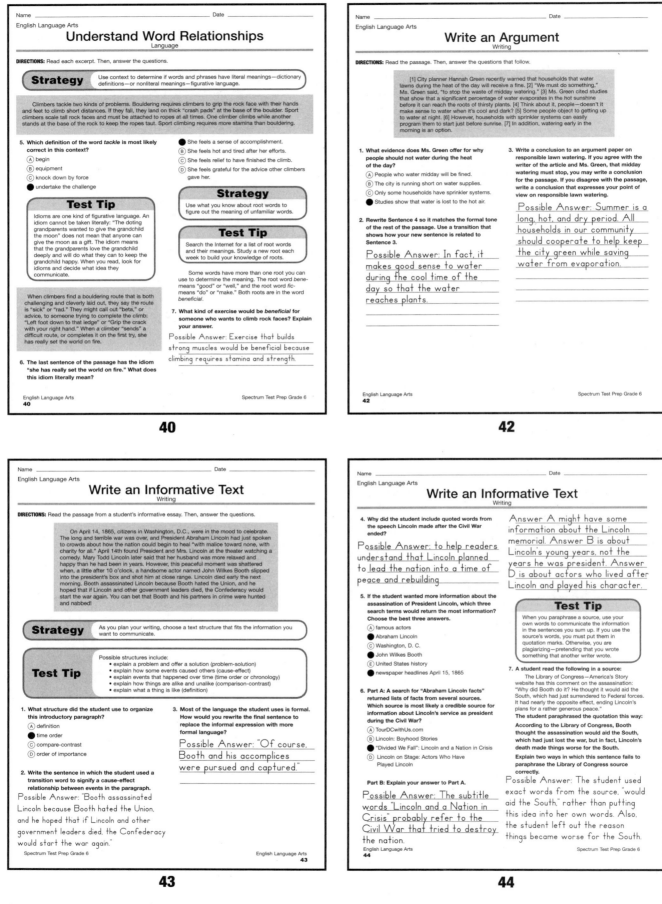

Understand Word Relationships
Language

DIRECTIONS: Read each excerpt. Then, answer the questions.

Strategy Use context to determine if words and phrases have literal meanings—dictionary definitions—or nonliteral meanings—figurative language.

Climbers tackle two kinds of problems. Bouldering requires climbers to grip the rock face with their hands and feet to climb short distances. If they fall, they land on thick "crash pads" at the base of the boulder. Sport climbers scale tall rock faces and must be attached to ropes at all times. One climber climbs while another stands at the base of the rock to keep the ropes taut. Sport climbing requires more stamina than bouldering.

5. Which definition of the word *tackle* is most likely correct in this context?
- (A) begin
- (B) equipment
- (C) knock down by force
- ● undertake the challenge

Test Tip

Idioms are one kind of figurative language. An idiom cannot be taken literally: "The doting grandparents wanted to give the grandchild the moon" does not mean that anyone can give the moon as a gift. The idiom means that the grandparents love the grandchild deeply and will do what they can to keep the grandchild happy. When you read, look for idioms and decide what idea they communicate.

When climbers find a bouldering route that is both challenging and cleverly laid out, they say the route is "sick" or "rad." They might call out "beta," or advice, to someone trying to complete the climb: "Left foot down to that ledge" or "Grip the crack with your right hand." When a climber "sends" a difficult route, or completes it on the first try, she has really set the world on fire.

6. The last sentence of the passage has the idiom "she has really set the world on fire." What does this idiom literally mean?

- (A) She feels a sense of accomplishment.
- (B) She feels hot and tired after her efforts.
- (C) She feels relief to have finished the climb.
- (D) She feels grateful for the advice other climbers gave her.

Strategy Use what you know about root words to figure out the meaning of unfamiliar words.

Test Tip

Search the Internet for a list of root words and their meanings. Study a new root each week to build your knowledge of roots.

Some words have more than one root you can use to determine the meaning. The root word *bene-* means "good" or "well," and the root word *fic-* means "do" or "make." Both roots are in the word *beneficial*.

7. What kind of exercise would be *beneficial* for someone who wants to climb rock faces? Explain your answer.

Possible Answer: Exercise that builds strong muscles would be beneficial because climbing requires stamina and strength.

40

Write an Argument
Writing

DIRECTIONS: Read the passage. Then, answer the questions that follow.

[1] City planner Hannah Green recently warned that households that water lawns during the heat of the day will waste water and face a fine. [2] "We must do something," Ms. Green said, "to stop the waste of midday watering." [3] Ms. Green cited studies that show that a significant percentage of water evaporates in the hot sunshine before it can reach the roots of thirsty plants. [4] Think about it, people—doesn't it make sense to water when it's cool and dark? [5] Some people object to getting up to water at night. [6] However, households with sprinkler systems can easily program them to start just before sunrise. [7] In addition, watering early in the morning is an option.

1. What evidence does Ms. Green offer for why people should not water during the heat of the day?
- (A) People who water midday will be fined.
- (B) The city is running short on water supplies.
- (C) Only some households have sprinkler systems.
- ● Studies show that water is lost to the hot air.

2. Rewrite Sentence 4 so it matches the formal tone of the rest of the passage. Use a transition that shows how your new sentence is related to Sentence 3.

Possible Answer: In fact, it makes good sense to water during the cool time of the day so that the water reaches plants.

3. Write a conclusion to an argument paper on responsible lawn watering. If you agree with the writer of the article and Ms. Green, that midday watering must stop, you may write a conclusion for the passage. If you disagree with the passage, write a conclusion that expresses your point of view on responsible lawn watering.

Possible Answer: Summer is a long, hot, and dry period. All households in our community should cooperate to help keep the city green while saving water from evaporation.

42

Write an Informative Text
Writing

DIRECTIONS: Read the passage from a student's informative essay. Then, answer the questions.

On April 14, 1865, citizens in Washington, D.C., were in the mood to celebrate. The long and terrible war was over, and President Abraham Lincoln had just spoken to crowds about how the nation could begin to heal "with malice toward none, with charity for all." April 14th found President and Mrs. Lincoln at the theater watching a comedy. Mary Todd Lincoln later said that her husband was more relaxed and happy than he had been in years. However, this peaceful moment was shattered when, a little after 10 o'clock, a handsome actor named John Wilkes Booth slipped into the president's box and shot him at close range. Lincoln died early the next morning. Booth assassinated Lincoln because Booth hated the Union, and he hoped that if Lincoln and other government leaders died, the Confederacy would start the war again. You can bet that Booth and his partners in crime were hunted and nabbed!

Strategy As you plan your writing, choose a text structure that fits the information you want to communicate.

Test Tip

Possible structures include:
- explain a problem and offer a solution (problem-solution)
- explain how some events caused others (cause-effect)
- explain events that happened over time (time order or chronology)
- explain how things are alike and unlike (comparison-contrast)
- explain what a thing is like (definition)

1. What structure did the student use to organize this introductory paragraph?
- (A) definition
- ● time order
- (C) compare-contrast
- (D) order of importance

2. Write the sentence in which the student used a transition word to signify a cause-effect relationship between events in the paragraph.

Possible Answer: "Booth assassinated Lincoln because Booth hated the Union, and he hoped that if Lincoln and other government leaders died, the Confederacy would start the war again."

3. Most of the language the student uses is formal. How would you rewrite the final sentence to replace the informal expression with more formal language?

Possible Answer: "Of course, Booth and his accomplices were pursued and captured."

43

Write an Informative Text
Writing

4. Why did the student include quoted words from the speech Lincoln made after the Civil War ended?

Possible Answer: to help readers understand that Lincoln planned to lead the nation into a time of peace and rebuilding

5. If the student wanted more information about the assassination of President Lincoln, which three search terms would return the most information? Choose the best three answers.
- (A) famous actors
- ● Abraham Lincoln
- (C) Washington, D. C.
- ● John Wilkes Booth
- (E) United States history
- ● newspaper headlines April 15, 1865

6. Part A: A search for "Abraham Lincoln facts" returned lists of facts from several sources. Which source is most likely a credible source for information about Lincoln's service as president during the Civil War?
- (A) TourDCwithUs.com
- (B) Lincoln: Boyhood Stories
- ● "Divided We Fall": Lincoln and a Nation in Crisis
- (D) Lincoln on Stage: Actors Who Have Played Lincoln

Part B: Explain your answer to Part A.

Possible Answer: The subtitle words "Lincoln and a Nation in Crisis" probably refer to the Civil War that tried to destroy the nation.

Answer A might have some information about the Lincoln memorial. Answer B is about Lincoln's young years, not the years he was president. Answer D is about actors who lived after Lincoln and played his character.

Test Tip

When you paraphrase a source, use your own words to communicate the information in the sentences you sum up. If you use the source's words, you must put them in quotation marks. Otherwise, you are plagiarizing—pretending that you wrote something that another writer wrote.

7. A student read the following in a source:
The Library of Congress—America's Story website has this comment on the assassination: "Why did Booth do it? He thought it would aid the South, which had just surrendered to Federal forces. It had nearly the opposite effect, ending Lincoln's plans for a rather generous peace."

The student paraphrased the quotation this way:
According to the Library of Congress, Booth thought the assassination would aid the South, which had just lost the war, but in fact, Lincoln's death made things worse for the South.

Explain two ways in which this sentence fails to paraphrase the Library of Congress source correctly.

Possible Answer: The student used exact words from the source, "would aid the South," rather than putting this idea into her own words. Also, the student left out the reason things became worse for the South.

44

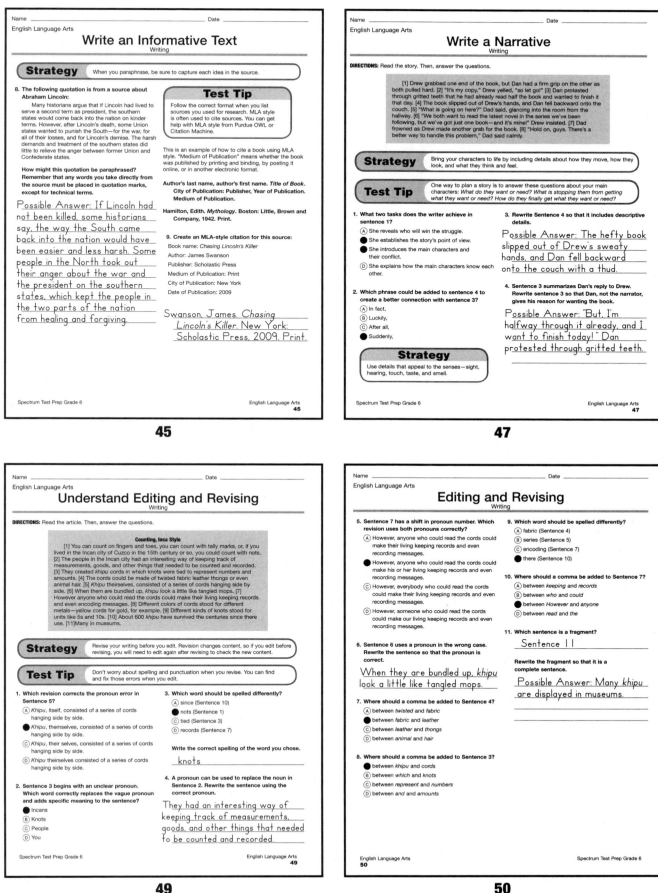

Write an Informative Text
Writing

Strategy When you paraphrase, be sure to capture each idea in the source.

8. The following quotation is from a source about Abraham Lincoln:

Many historians argue that if Lincoln had lived to serve a second term as president, the southern states would come back into the nation on kinder terms. However, after Lincoln's death, some Union states wanted to punish the South—for the war, for all of their losses, and for Lincoln's demise. The harsh demands and treatment of the southern states did little to relieve the anger between former Union and Confederate states.

How might this quotation be paraphrased? Remember that any words you take directly from the source must be placed in quotation marks, except for technical terms.

Possible Answer: If Lincoln had not been killed, some historians say, the way the South came back into the nation would have been easier and less harsh. Some people in the North took out their anger about the war and the president on the southern states, which kept the people in the two parts of the nation from healing and forgiving.

Test Tip
Follow the correct format when you list sources you used for research. MLA style is often used to cite sources. You can get help with MLA style from Purdue OWL or Citation Machine.

This is an example of how to cite a book using MLA style. "Medium of Publication" means whether the book was published by printing and binding, by posting it online, or in another electronic format.

Author's last name, author's first name. *Title of Book.* City of Publication: Publisher, Year of Publication. Medium of Publication.

Hamilton, Edith. *Mythology.* Boston: Little, Brown and Company, 1942. Print.

9. Create an MLA-style citation for this source:
Book name: *Chasing Lincoln's Killer*
Author: James Swanson
Publisher: Scholastic Press
Medium of Publication: Print
City of Publication: New York
Date of Publication: 2009

Swanson, James. *Chasing Lincoln's Killer.* New York: Scholastic Press, 2009. Print.

45

Write a Narrative
Writing

DIRECTIONS: Read the story. Then, answer the questions.

[1] Drew grabbed one end of the book, but Dan had a firm grip on the other as both pulled hard. [2] "It's my copy," Drew yelled, "so let go!" [3] Dan protested through gritted teeth that he had already read half the book and wanted to finish it that day. [4] The book slipped out of Drew's hands, and Dan fell backward onto the couch. [5] "What is going on here?" Dad said, glancing into the room from the hallway. [6] "We both want to read the latest novel in the series we've been following, but we've got just one book—and it's mine!" Drew insisted. [7] Dad frowned as Drew made another grab for the book. [8] "Hold on, guys. There's a better way to handle this problem," Dad said calmly.

Strategy Bring your characters to life by including details about how they move, how they look, and what they think and feel.

Test Tip One way to plan a story is to answer these questions about your main characters: *What do they want or need? What is stopping them from getting what they want or need? How do they finally get what they want or need?*

1. What two tasks does the writer achieve in sentence 1?
   - (A) She reveals who will win the struggle.
   - ● She establishes the story's point of view.
   - ● She introduces the main characters and their conflict.
   - (D) She explains how the main characters know each other.

2. Which phrase could be added to sentence 4 to create a better connection with sentence 3?
   - (A) In fact,
   - (B) Luckily,
   - (C) After all,
   - ● Suddenly,

Strategy
Use details that appeal to the senses—sight, hearing, touch, taste, and smell.

3. Rewrite Sentence 4 so that it includes descriptive details.

Possible Answer: The hefty book slipped out of Drew's sweaty hands, and Dan fell backward onto the couch with a thud.

4. Sentence 3 summarizes Dan's reply to Drew. Rewrite sentence 3 so that Dan, not the narrator, gives his reason for wanting the book.

Possible Answer: "But, I'm halfway through it already, and I want to finish today!" Dan protested through gritted teeth.

47

Understand Editing and Revising
Writing

DIRECTIONS: Read the article. Then, answer the questions.

Counting, Inca Style
[1] You can count on fingers and toes, you can count with tally marks, or, if you lived in the Incan city of Cuzco in the 15th century or so, you could count with nots. [2] The people in the Incan city had an interesting way of keeping track of measurements, goods, and other things that needed to be counted and recorded. [3] They created *khipu* cords in which knots were tied to represent numbers and amounts. [4] The cords could be made of twisted fabric leather thongs or even animal hair. [5] *Khipu* theirselves, consisted of a series of cords hanging side by side. [6] When them are bundled up, *khipu* look a little like tangled mops. [7] However anyone who could read the cords could make their living keeping records and even encoding messages. [8] Different colors of cords stood for different metals—yellow cords for gold, for example. [9] Different kinds of knots stood for units like 5s and 10s. [10] About 600 *khipu* have survived the centuries since there use. [11] Many in museums.

Strategy Revise your writing before you edit. Revision changes content, so if you edit before revising, you will need to edit again after revising to check the new content.

Test Tip Don't worry about spelling and punctuation when you revise. You can find and fix those errors when you edit.

1. Which revision corrects the pronoun error in Sentence 5?
   - (A) *Khipu,* itself, consisted of a series of cords hanging side by side.
   - ● *Khipu,* themselves, consisted of a series of cords hanging side by side.
   - (C) *Khipu,* their selves, consisted of a series of cords hanging side by side.
   - (D) *Khipu* theirselves consisted of a series of cords hanging side by side.

2. Sentence 3 begins with an unclear pronoun. Which word correctly replaces the vague pronoun and adds specific meaning to the sentence?
   - ● Incans
   - (B) Knots
   - (C) People
   - (D) You

3. Which word should be spelled differently?
   - (A) since (Sentence 10)
   - ● nots (Sentence 1)
   - (C) tied (Sentence 3)
   - (D) records (Sentence 7)

Write the correct spelling of the word you chose.
knots

4. A pronoun can be used to replace the noun in Sentence 2. Rewrite the sentence using the correct pronoun.

They had an interesting way of keeping track of measurements, goods, and other things that needed to be counted and recorded.

49

Editing and Revising
Writing

5. Sentence 7 has a shift in pronoun number. Which revision uses both pronouns correctly?
   - (A) However, anyone who could read the cords could make their living keeping records and even recording messages.
   - ● However, anyone who could read the cords could make his or her living keeping records and even recording messages.
   - (C) However, everybody who could read the cords could make their living keeping records and even recording messages.
   - (D) However, someone who could read the cords could make our living keeping records and even recording messages.

6. Sentence 6 uses a pronoun in the wrong case. Rewrite the sentence so that the pronoun is correct.

When they are bundled up, *khipu* look a little like tangled mops.

7. Where should a comma be added to Sentence 4?
   - (A) between *twisted* and *fabric*
   - ● between *fabric* and *leather*
   - (C) between *leather* and *thongs*
   - (D) between *animal* and *hair*

8. Where should a comma be added to Sentence 3?
   - ● between *khipu* and *cords*
   - (B) between *which* and *knots*
   - (C) between *represent* and *numbers*
   - (D) between *and* and *amounts*

9. Which word should be spelled differently?
   - (A) fabric (Sentence 4)
   - (B) series (Sentence 5)
   - (C) encoding (Sentence 7)
   - ● there (Sentence 10)

10. Where should a comma be added to Sentence 7?
   - (A) between *keeping* and *records*
   - (B) between *who* and *could*
   - ● between *However* and *anyone*
   - (D) between *read* and *the*

11. Which sentence is a fragment?
Sentence 11

Rewrite the fragment so that it is a complete sentence.

Possible Answer: Many *khipu* are displayed in museums.

50

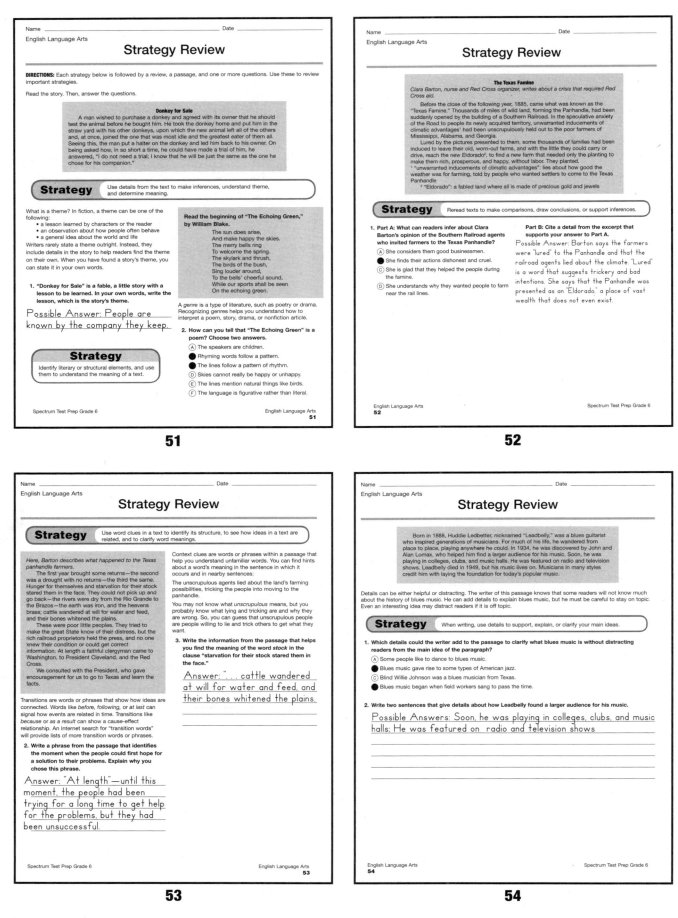

Page 51

Strategy Review

DIRECTIONS: Each strategy below is followed by a review, a passage, and one or more questions. Use these to review important strategies.

Read the story. Then, answer the questions.

Donkey for Sale

A man wished to purchase a donkey and agreed with its owner that he should test the animal before he bought him. He took the donkey home and put him in the straw yard with his other donkeys, upon which the new animal left all of the others and, at once, joined the one that was most idle and the greatest eater of them all. Seeing this, the man put a halter on the donkey and led him back to his owner. On being asked how, in so short a time, he could have made a trial of him, he answered, "I do not need a trial; I know that he will be just the same as the one he chose for his companion."

Strategy — Use details from the text to make inferences, understand theme, and determine meaning.

What is a theme? In fiction, a theme can be one of the following:
• a lesson learned by characters or the reader
• an observation about how people often behave
• a general idea about the world and life

Writers rarely state a theme outright. Instead, they include details in the story to help readers find the theme on their own. When you have found a story's theme, you can state it in your own words.

1. "Donkey for Sale" is a fable, a little story with a lesson to be learned. In your own words, write the lesson, which is the story's theme.

Possible Answer: People are known by the company they keep.

Strategy — Identify literary or structural elements, and use them to understand the meaning of a text.

Read the beginning of "The Echoing Green," by William Blake.

The sun does arise,
And make happy the skies.
The merry bells ring
To welcome the spring.
The skylark and thrush,
The birds of the bush,
Sing louder around,
To the bells' cheerful sound,
While our sports shall be seen
On the echoing green.

A *genre* is a type of literature, such as poetry or drama. Recognizing genres helps you understand how to interpret a poem, story, drama, or nonfiction article.

2. How can you tell that "The Echoing Green" is a poem? Choose two answers.
(A) The speakers are children.
● Rhyming words follow a pattern.
● The lines follow a pattern of rhythm.
(D) Skies cannot really be happy or unhappy.
(E) The lines mention natural things like birds.
(F) The language is figurative rather than literal.

51

Page 52

Strategy Review

The Texas Famine
Clara Barton, nurse and Red Cross organizer, writes about a crisis that required Red Cross aid.

Before the close of the following year, 1885, came what was known as the "Texas Famine." Thousands of miles of wild land, forming the Panhandle, had been suddenly opened by the building of a Southern Railroad. In the speculative anxiety of the Road to people its newly acquired territory, unwarranted inducements of climatic advantages[1] had been unscrupulously held out to the poor farmers of Mississippi, Alabama, and Georgia.

Lured by the pictures presented to them, some thousands of families had been induced to leave their old, worn-out farms, and with the little they could carry or drive, reach the new Eldorado[2], to find a new farm that needed only the planting to make them rich, prosperous, and happy, without labor. They planted.
[1] "unwarranted inducements of climatic advantages": lies about how good the weather was for farming, told by people who wanted settlers to come to the Texas Panhandle
[2] "Eldorado": a fabled land where all is made of precious gold and jewels

Strategy — Reread texts to make comparisons, draw conclusions, or support inferences.

1. **Part A:** What can readers infer about Clara Barton's opinion of the Southern Railroad agents who invited farmers to the Texas Panhandle?
(A) She considers them good businessmen.
● She finds their actions dishonest and cruel.
(C) She is glad that they helped the people during the famine.
(D) She understands why they wanted people to farm near the rail lines.

Part B: Cite a detail from the excerpt that supports your answer to Part A.

Possible Answer: Barton says the farmers were "lured" to the Panhandle and that the railroad agents lied about the climate. "Lured" is a word that suggests trickery and bad intentions. She says that the Panhandle was presented as an "Eldorado," a place of vast wealth that does not even exist.

52

Page 53

Strategy Review

Strategy — Use word clues in a text to identify its structure, to see how ideas in a text are related, and to clarify word meanings.

Here, Barton describes what happened to the Texas panhandle farmers.

The first year brought some returns—the second was a drought with no returns—the third the same. Hunger for themselves and starvation for their stock stared them in the face. They could not pick up and go back—the rivers were dry from the Rio Grande to the Brazos—the earth was iron, and the heavens brass; cattle wandered at will for water and feed, and their bones whitened the plains.

These were poor little peoples. They tried to make the great State know of their distress, but the rich railroad proprietors held the press, and no one knew their condition or could get correct information. At length a faithful clergyman came to Washington, to President Cleveland, and the Red Cross.

We consulted with the President, who gave encouragement for us to go to Texas and learn the facts.

Transitions are words or phrases that show how ideas are connected. Words like *before, following,* or *at last* can signal how events are related in time. Transitions like *because* or *as a result* can show a cause-effect relationship. An Internet search for "transition words" will provide lists of more transition words or phrases.

2. Write a phrase from the passage that identifies the moment when the people could first hope for a solution to their problems. Explain why you chose this phrase.

Answer: "At length"—until this moment, the people had been trying for a long time to get help for the problems, but they had been unsuccessful.

Context clues are words or phrases within a passage that help you understand unfamiliar words. You can find hints about a word's meaning in the sentence in which it occurs and in nearby sentences:

The unscrupulous agents lied about the land's farming possibilities, tricking the people into moving to the panhandle.

You may not know what *unscrupulous* means, but you probably know what lying and tricking are and why they are wrong. So, you can guess that unscrupulous people are people willing to lie and trick others to get what they want.

3. Write the information from the passage that helps you find the meaning of the word *stock* in the clause "starvation for their stock stared them in the face."

Answer: "... cattle wandered at will for water and feed, and their bones whitened the plains."

53

Page 54

Strategy Review

Born in 1888, Huddie Ledbetter, nicknamed "Leadbelly," was a blues guitarist who inspired generations of musicians. For much of his life, he wandered from place to place, playing anywhere he could. In 1934, he was discovered by John and Alan Lomax, who helped him find a larger audience for his music. Soon, he was playing in colleges, clubs, and music halls. He was featured on radio and television shows. Leadbelly died in 1949, but his music lives on. Musicians in many styles credit him with laying the foundation for today's popular music.

Details can be either helpful or distracting. The writer of this passage knows that some readers will not know much about the history of blues music. He can add details to explain blues music, but he must be careful to stay on topic. Even an interesting idea may distract readers if it is off topic.

Strategy — When writing, use details to support, explain, or clarify your main ideas.

1. Which details could the writer add to the passage to clarify what blues music is without distracting readers from the main idea of the paragraph?
(A) Some people like to dance to blues music.
● Blues music gave rise to some types of American jazz.
(C) Blind Willie Johnson was a blues musician from Texas.
● Blues music began when field workers sang to pass the time.

2. Write two sentences that give details about how Leadbelly found a larger audience for his music.

Possible Answers: Soon, he was playing in colleges, clubs, and music halls; He was featured on radio and television shows

54

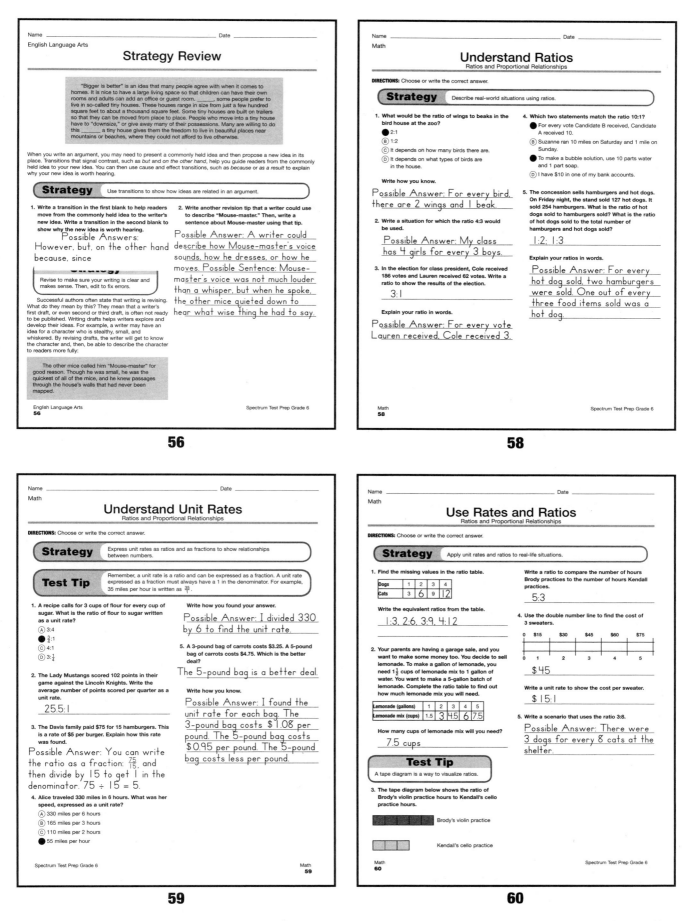

56

58

59

60

Use Rates and Ratios
Ratios and Proportional Relationships

DIRECTIONS: Choose or write the correct answer.

Strategy Use ratios and rates to express comparisons and make decisions.

6. A cheetah can run up to 60 miles per hour. Which equation shows how fast a cheetah could run in 45 minutes?
   (A) 60 × 45 = 2,700
   (B) 60 ÷ 12 = 1.33
   ● $\frac{3}{4}$ × 60 = 45
   (D) $\frac{60}{45}$ × 60 = 80

7. Caroline looked at a website to buy dog food. The website she looked at sells three different brands. Use the table to decide which brand is the best value.

Brand	Puppy Protein	Delicious Dog Food	YUM Dog Food
Size	14 pounds	17 pounds	15 pounds
Price	$17.50	$19.55	$19.50

Delicious Dog Food is the best deal.

Explain how you know your answer is correct.

Possible Answer: I divided the price by the number of pounds for each brand to find how much each food cost per pound. Then, I chose the brand with the lowest cost per pound.

8. U.S. nuclear submarines can travel 25 nautical miles per hour under water. Complete the table to show how far a submarine can travel in 5, 10, and 15 hours.

Nautical Miles	25	125	250	375
Hour	1	5	10	15

9. A box of cereal has a calorie-to-serving ratio of 114:1. If a serving is one cup, how many calories are there in 3$\frac{1}{2}$ cups of the cereal?
   (A) 32.57
   (B) 117.5
   ● 399
   (D) 342

10. Write a scenario that uses the ratio 4:7.

Possible Answer: I made a snack using 4 crackers and 7 pieces of cheese.

61

Use Percents
Ratios and Proportional Relationships

DIRECTIONS: Choose or write the correct answer.

Strategy Use multiplication, division, and proportions to find answers to percent problems.

1. What is 62% of 72?
   ● 44.64
   (B) 0.009
   (C) 4,464
   (D) 10

2. What is 73% of 87?
   (A) 20
   (B) 6,351
   (C) 0.839
   ● 63.51

3. Write each fraction as a percent.
   60%
   67%
   63%
   86%

4. Write each fraction as a percent.
   80%
   37.5%
   167%
   78%

Strategy
The proportion $\frac{a}{b} = \frac{p}{100}$ can help you find the answer to percent problems.

5. Pizzazz Pizza Parlor gave the sixth-grade class a 25% discount on pizzas they purchased for a party. Each pizza originally cost $12.00. How much did the sixth graders pay per pizza?
   (A) $3.00
   ● $9.00
   (C) $8.00
   (D) $6.00

6. Twenty-five percent of the workers are on third shift. There are 33 workers on third shift. How many workers are there total? Show your work.

$\frac{a}{b} = \frac{p}{100}; \frac{33}{b} = \frac{25}{100}:$

$3,300 \div 25 = b$

$= 132$

7. Forty percent of the members of the drama club are boys. There are 55 members of drama club. How many are girls? Show your work.

$0.60 \times 55 = 33;33$ members are girls.

62

Convert Measurement Units
Ratios and Proportional Relationships

DIRECTIONS: Choose or write the correct answer.

Strategy Convert from one unit to another using proportions.

Test Tip Use the equivalency table to help you create your proportions.

1 gallon = 4 quarts	1 foot = 12 inches
2 pints = 1 quart	1 centimeter = 10 millimeters
2 cups = 1 pint	1 kilogram = 1,000 grams
8 fluid ounces = 1 cup	1 gram = 1,000 milligrams
1 yard = 3 feet	

1. A recipe calls for 6 quarts of water. How many gallons is that?
   (A) 1 gallon
   ● 1$\frac{1}{2}$ gallons
   (C) 2 gallons
   (D) 2$\frac{1}{2}$ gallons

2. Kenny's book is 30 millimeters thick. How many centimeters thick is the book?

   3 cm

3. A football field is 100 yards long. Use proportions to find out how many inches long a football field is.

$\frac{100}{x} = \frac{1}{3}; \frac{300}{x} = \frac{1}{12}; 3,600$ inches

4. Sixteen cups is equivalent to all of the following except _____?
   (A) 8 pints
   (B) 1 gallon
   (C) 4 quarts
   ● 100 fluid ounces

5. A gallon of milk costs $3.25. How much does it cost per 1-cup serving? Show your work.

$\frac{3.25}{16} = 0.20$

$0.20

63

Divide Fractions
The Number System

DIRECTIONS: Choose or write the correct answer.

Strategy Use multiplication to divide fractions.

Test Tip Remember to multiply by the reciprocal when dividing fractions.

1. $\frac{2}{3} \div \frac{4}{3} =$ _____ Show your work.

$\frac{2}{3} \times \frac{4}{3} = \frac{8}{9}$

2. Explain the steps for dividing fractions.

Possible Answer: To divide fractions, you have to multiply the dividend by the reciprocal of the divisor first. Then, the quotient needs to be reduced to simplest form.

Show an example of the steps you described.

Possible Answer:
$\frac{2}{5} \div \frac{4}{7}; \frac{2}{5} \times \frac{7}{4} = \frac{14}{20} = \frac{7}{10}$

3. Brody made $\frac{7}{8}$ pound of granola. If he puts $\frac{1}{4}$ pound of granola into each bag, how many bags will he be able to fill completely?
   ● 3
   (B) 3$\frac{1}{2}$
   (C) 4
   (D) 4$\frac{1}{2}$

Write how you found your answer.

Possible Answer: I divided $\frac{7}{8}$ by $\frac{1}{4}$ to find how many bags were filled. The answer was 3$\frac{1}{2}$, so I know only 3 bags could be filled completely.

4. Mr. Rodriguez bought a 1$\frac{1}{2}$ pound tub of popcorn. He divided it equally among his 4 children. How much popcorn did each child get? Which two expressions could be used to solve this problem?
   ● $\frac{3}{2} \times \frac{1}{4}$
   (B) 4 ÷ $\frac{3}{2}$
   (C) 4 × $\frac{3}{2}$
   ● $\frac{3}{2} \div 4$

64

Page 65

Math

Divide Fractions
The Number System

DIRECTIONS: Choose or write the correct answer.

Strategy Divide fractions to solve real-world problems.

5. How many $\frac{1}{3}$ cup servings are in $\frac{3}{4}$ cup of yogurt?
- ● $2\frac{1}{4}$
- (B) $\frac{1}{12}$
- (C) $\frac{1}{3}$
- (D) $\frac{4}{7}$

9. How much chocolate candy will each child get if 3 children share a $\frac{1}{4}$ pound bag of chocolate candies?

$\frac{1}{12}$ pound

6. What is the area of a canyon with a length of $\frac{1}{2}$ mile and a width of 2.25 miles? Show your work.

$1\frac{1}{8}$ miles

Draw a visual fraction model to illustrate your answer.

Possible Answer: $\frac{1}{12}$ pound

7. How long is a park with a width of $\frac{3}{4}$ mile and an area of 1.5 square miles? Show your work.

2 miles

8. Brooke ran for $\frac{2}{3}$ hour. She ran a total of $2\frac{1}{3}$ miles. What was her speed in miles per hour? Show your work.

$3\frac{1}{2}$ miles per hour

10. What is the area of a field with a length of $\frac{3}{4}$ mile and a width of 2.5 miles? Show your work.

$1\frac{7}{8}$ miles

Spectrum Test Prep Grade 6

Math
65

Page 66

Math

Divide Multi-Digit Numbers
The Number System

DIRECTIONS: Choose or write the correct answer.

Strategy Follow the steps of long division to complete long division with multi-digit numbers.

Test Tip Remember to follow the steps of standard division: Divide, Multiply, Subtract, Bring Down, Repeat.

1. 4,281 ÷ 3 = _____

1,427

Write how you know.

Possible Answer: I divided 450 by 18 to get 25.

2. A student completed the division problem below. Explain the student's error and give the correct quotient.

```
      21
32)6848
    - 64
      44
    - 32
      28
```

The quotient is 21 r28.

Possible Answer: In the last subtraction step, the student did not complete 4 − 3. If he had done that, the result would have been 128, which would give a quotient of 214.

3. A pet store has 450 goldfish. They want to divide the fish equally into 18 tanks. How many goldfish should they put in each tank?
- (A) 8,100
- (B) 432
- ● 25
- (D) 468

4. The Mason family is planning a summer road trip. They want to travel for 14 days, for a total distance of 2,317 miles. How many miles should they travel each day?
- (A) 166
- (B) 165
- (C) 165 r7
- ● 165.5

5. Ms. Raphael is pouring lemonade into cups for a party. She begins with 4,000 mL. She pours 280 mL into each cup. How many cups can she fill? Explain how you found your answer.

Possible Answer: She can fill 14 cups; 4,000 divided by 280 is about 14.29, so she can fill 14 cups and will have a little left over.

Math
66

Spectrum Test Prep Grade 6

Page 67

Math

Compute with Decimals
The Number System

DIRECTIONS: Choose or write the correct answer.

Strategy Look for key words in word problems that help you determine which operation to use.

1. The average annual temperature in Death Valley, California is 77.2°F. The average annual temperature in Anchorage, Alaska is 37°F. On average, how much warmer is it in Death Valley than in Anchorage?

40.2°F

Write why you chose the operation you did.

Possible Answer: The question is looking for a difference in temperature. To find a difference, you subtract.

2. According to the nutritional information on the box, a serving of crackers has 3.5 grams of fat. If there are 9 crackers in a serving, how many grams of fat would be in each cracker?
- (A) about 12.5 grams
- (B) about 6.5 grams
- ● about 0.39 grams
- (D) about 31.5 grams

Write why you chose the operation you did.

Possible Answer: The question is looking for the amount of fat per cracker. Thus, I must divide the fat equally among the crackers.

3. A flight attendant flew 4 flights in 3 days. On Monday, she flew 1,275.3 miles. On Tuesday, she flew 514.5 miles. On Wednesday, she flew two flights. One flight was 2,050.15 miles, and the other was 362.175 miles. How many miles did she accumulate during the 3 days?

4,202.125 miles

4. Sean's car gets 36.9 miles per gallon. How many gallons of gas would Sean need to travel 250 miles?
- (A) 9,225
- ● 6.8
- (C) 0.148
- (D) 286.9

If gas costs $3.29 per gallon, how much will it cost Sean to make this trip? Show your work.

$22.37

Spectrum Test Prep Grade 6

Math
67

Page 68

Math

Compute with Decimals
The Number System

DIRECTIONS: Choose or write the correct answer.

Strategy Use basic operations to solve real-world problems involving money.

5. Else, Sienna, and Alexa bought a gift for their mother. The total price for the gift was $112.32. How much did each sister pay if they split the total evenly? Show your work.

$37.44

6. Explain the error and give the correct product.

```
      27.4
   × 1.36
     1644
     8220
  + 27400
   372.64
```

Possible Answer: The product should be 37.264. The student did not count all of the decimal places in the original problem.

7. Jeremiah received a $50 gift card for a video game store. He purchased Krazy Karts for $29.99, Sumo Superstar for $27.50, and a new controller for $15.99. The tax came to $4.41. After using the gift card, how much did Jeremiah have to pay?
- (A) $77.89
- (B) $17.89
- (C) $127.89
- ● $27.89

Write how you know.

Possible Answer: I first added all the prices to get the total bill. Then, I subtracted the $50 gift card to get what he would have to pay.

8. Reese went back-to-school shopping. She bought 3 sweaters at $19.99 each, 4 pairs of jeans at 2 for $50.50, and a pair of shoes for $75.25. Her mother agreed to pay for half the clothing bill. How much did Reese pay? Show your work.

$118.11

9. A family drove 358.15 miles on Friday. On, Saturday, they drove 426.3 miles. On Sunday, they drove 504.5 miles. How many miles did they drive in all?

1288.95 miles

Math
68

Spectrum Test Prep Grade 6

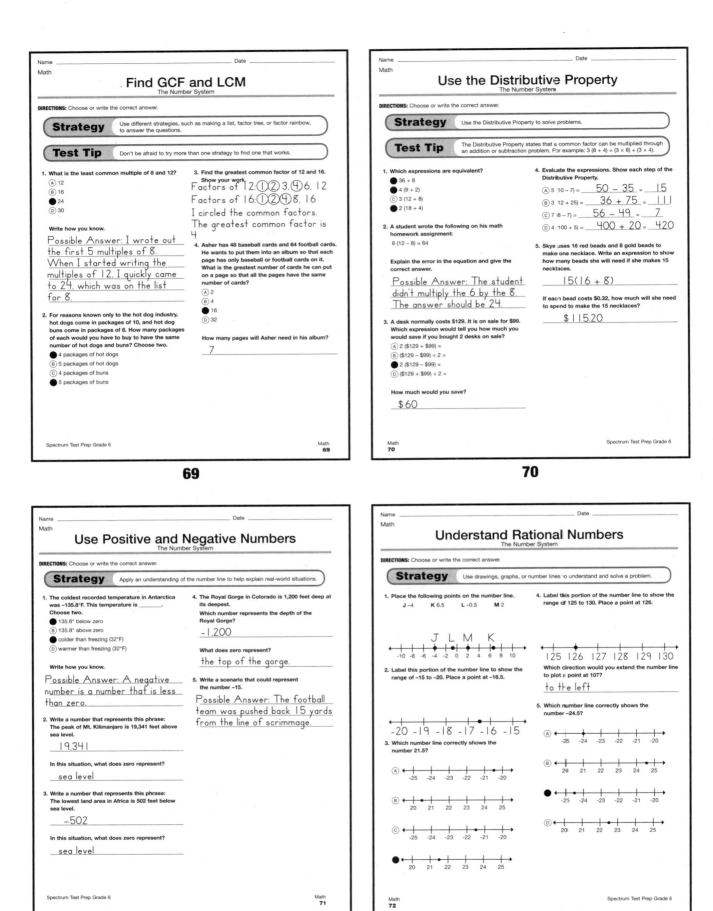

Find GCF and LCM
The Number System

DIRECTIONS: Choose or write the correct answer.

Strategy Use different strategies, such as making a list, factor tree, or factor rainbow, to answer the questions.

Test Tip Don't be afraid to try more than one strategy to find one that works.

1. What is the least common multiple of 8 and 12?
   (A) 12
   (B) 16
   ● 24
   (D) 30

Write how you know.

Possible Answer: I wrote out the first 5 multiples of 8. When I started writing the multiples of 12, I quickly came to 24, which was on the list for 8.

2. For reasons known only to the hot dog industry, hot dogs come in packages of 10, and hot dog buns come in packages of 8. How many packages of each would you have to buy to have the same number of hot dogs and buns? Choose two.
   ● 4 packages of hot dogs
   (B) 5 packages of hot dogs
   (C) 4 packages of buns
   ● 5 packages of buns

3. Find the greatest common factor of 12 and 16. Show your work.
   Factors of 12: ①②3 ④ 6, 12
   Factors of 16: ①②④8, 16
   I circled the common factors. The greatest common factor is 4.

4. Asher has 48 baseball cards and 64 football cards. He wants to put them into an album so that each page has only baseball or football cards on it. What is the greatest number of cards he can put on a page so that all the pages have the same number of cards?
   (A) 2
   (B) 4
   ● 16
   (D) 32

How many pages will Asher need in his album?
   7

Spectrum Test Prep Grade 6

Math
69

Use the Distributive Property
The Number System

DIRECTIONS: Choose or write the correct answer.

Strategy Use the Distributive Property to solve problems.

Test Tip The Distributive Property states that a common factor can be multiplied through an addition or subtraction problem. For example: 3 (8 + 4) = (3 × 8) + (3 × 4).

1. Which expressions are equivalent?
   ● 36 + 8
   ● 4 (9 + 2)
   (C) 3 (12 + 8)
   ● 2 (18 + 4)

2. A student wrote the following on his math homework assignment:
   6 (12 − 8) = 64
   Explain the error in the equation and give the correct answer.
   Possible Answer: The student didn't multiply the 6 by the 8. The answer should be 24.

3. A desk normally costs $129. It is on sale for $99. Which expression would tell you how much you would save if you bought 2 desks on sale?
   (A) 2 ($129 + $99) =
   (B) ($129 − $99) ÷ 2 =
   ● 2 ($129 − $99) =
   (D) ($129 + $99) ÷ 2 =

How much would you save?
   $60

4. Evaluate the expressions. Show each step of the Distributive Property.
   (A) 5 (10 − 7) = __50 − 35 = 15__
   (B) 3 (12 + 25) = __36 + 75 = 111__
   (C) 7 (8 − 7) = __56 − 49 = 7__
   (D) 4 (100 + 5) = __400 + 20 = 420__

5. Skye uses 16 red beads and 8 gold beads to make one necklace. Write an expression to show how many beads she will need if she makes 15 necklaces.
   15 (16 + 8)
   If each bead costs $0.32, how much will she need to spend to make the 15 necklaces?
   $115.20

Math
70
Spectrum Test Prep Grade 6

Use Positive and Negative Numbers
The Number System

DIRECTIONS: Choose or write the correct answer.

Strategy Apply an understanding of the number line to help explain real-world situations.

1. The coldest recorded temperature in Antarctica was −135.8°F. This temperature is _____. Choose two.
   ● 135.8° below zero
   (B) 135.8° above zero
   ● colder than freezing (32°F)
   (D) warmer than freezing (32°F)

Write how you know.
   Possible Answer: A negative number is a number that is less than zero.

2. Write a number that represents this phrase: The peak of Mt. Kilimanjaro is 19,341 feet above sea level.
   19,341
   In this situation, what does zero represent?
   sea level

3. Write a number that represents this phrase: The lowest land area in Africa is 502 feet below sea level.
   −502
   In this situation, what does zero represent?
   sea level

4. The Royal Gorge in Colorado is 1,200 feet deep at its deepest. Which number represents the depth of the Royal Gorge?
   −1,200
   What does zero represent?
   the top of the gorge.

5. Write a scenario that could represent the number −15.
   Possible Answer: The football team was pushed back 15 yards from the line of scrimmage.

Spectrum Test Prep Grade 6

Math
71

Understand Rational Numbers
The Number System

DIRECTIONS: Choose or write the correct answer.

Strategy Use drawings, graphs, or number lines to understand and solve a problem.

1. Place the following points on the number line.
   J −4   K 6.5   L −0.5   M 2

2. Label this portion of the number line to show the range of −15 to −20. Place a point at −16.5.

3. Which number line correctly shows the number 21.5?
   (A)
   (B)
   (C)
   ●

4. Label this portion of the number line to show the range of 125 to 130. Place a point at 126.

Which direction would you extend the number line to plot a point at 107?
   to the left

5. Which number line correctly shows the number −24.5?
   (A)
   (B)
   ●
   (D)

Math
72
Spectrum Test Prep Grade 6

Answer Key
120

Spectrum Test Prep Grade 6

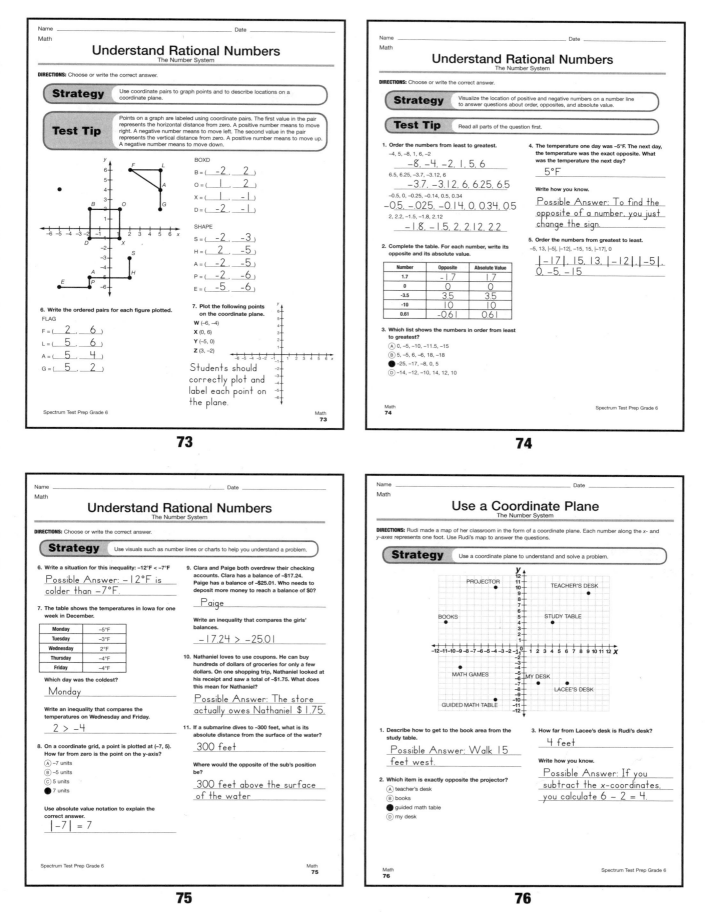

Understand Rational Numbers
The Number System

DIRECTIONS: Choose or write the correct answer.

Strategy Use coordinate pairs to graph points and to describe locations on a coordinate plane.

Test Tip Points on a graph are labeled using coordinate pairs. The first value in the pair represents the horizontal distance from zero. A positive number means to move right. A negative number means to move left. The second value in the pair represents the vertical distance from zero. A positive number means to move up. A negative number means to move down.

BOXD
B = (-2 , 2)
O = (1 , 2)
X = (1 , -1)
D = (-2 , -1)

SHAPE
S = (-2 , -3)
H = (2 , -5)
A = (-2 , -5)
P = (-2 , -6)
E = (-5 , -6)

6. Write the ordered pairs for each figure plotted.

FLAG
F = (2 , 6)
L = (5 , 6)
A = (5 , 4)
G = (5 , 2)

7. Plot the following points on the coordinate plane.
W (–6, –4)
X (0, 6)
Y (–5, 0)
Z (3, –2)

Students should correctly plot and label each point on the plane.

73

Understand Rational Numbers
The Number System

DIRECTIONS: Choose or write the correct answer.

Strategy Visualize the location of positive and negative numbers on a number line to answer questions about order, opposites, and absolute value.

Test Tip Read all parts of the question first.

1. Order the numbers from least to greatest.
–4, 5, –8, 1, 6, –2
–8, –4, –2, 1, 5, 6
6.5, 6.25, –3.7, –3.12, 6
–3.7, –3.12, 6, 6.25, 6.5
–0.5, 0, –0.25, –0.14, 0.5, 0.34
–0.5, –0.25, –0.14, 0, 0.34, 0.5
2, 2.2, –1.5, –1.8, 2.12
–1.8, –1.5, 2, 2.12, 2.2

2. Complete the table. For each number, write its opposite and its absolute value.

Number	Opposite	Absolute Value
1.7	–1.7	1.7
0	0	0
-3.5	3.5	3.5
-10	10	10
0.61	–0.61	0.61

3. Which list shows the numbers in order from least to greatest?
Ⓐ 0, –5, –10, –11.5, –15
Ⓑ 5, –5, 6, –6, 18, –18
● –25, –17, –8, 0, 5
Ⓓ –14, –12, –10, 14, 12, 10

4. The temperature one day was –5°F. The next day, the temperature was the exact opposite. What was the temperature the next day?
5°F

Write how you know.
Possible Answer: To find the opposite of a number, you just change the sign.

5. Order the numbers from greatest to least.
–5, 13, |–5|, |–12|, –15, 15, |–17|, 0
|–17|, 15, 13, |–12|, |–5|, 0, –5, –15

74

Understand Rational Numbers
The Number System

DIRECTIONS: Choose or write the correct answer.

Strategy Use visuals such as number lines or charts to help you understand a problem.

6. Write a situation for this inequality: –12°F < –7°F
Possible Answer: –12°F is colder than –7°F.

7. The table shows the temperatures in Iowa for one week in December.

Monday	–5°F
Tuesday	–3°F
Wednesday	2°F
Thursday	–4°F
Friday	–4°F

Which day was the coldest?
Monday

Write an inequality that compares the temperatures on Wednesday and Friday.
2 > –4

8. On a coordinate grid, a point is plotted at (–7, 5). How far from zero is the point on the y-axis?
Ⓐ –7 units
Ⓑ –5 units
Ⓒ 5 units
● 7 units

Use absolute value notation to explain the correct answer.
|–7| = 7

9. Clara and Paige both overdrew their checking accounts. Clara has a balance of –$17.24. Paige has a balance of –$25.01. Who needs to deposit more money to reach a balance of $0?
Paige

Write an inequality that compares the girls' balances.
–17.24 > –25.01

10. Nathaniel loves to use coupons. He can buy hundreds of dollars of groceries for only a few dollars. On one shopping trip, Nathaniel looked at his receipt and saw a total of –$1.75. What does this mean for Nathaniel?
Possible Answer: The store actually owes Nathaniel $1.75.

11. If a submarine dives to –300 feet, what is its absolute distance from the surface of the water?
300 feet

Where would the opposite of the sub's position be?
300 feet above the surface of the water

75

Use a Coordinate Plane
The Number System

DIRECTIONS: Rudi made a map of her classroom in the form of a coordinate plane. Each number along the x- and y-axes represents one foot. Use Rudi's map to answer the questions.

Strategy Use a coordinate plane to understand and solve a problem.

1. Describe how to get to the book area from the study table.
Possible Answer: Walk 15 feet west.

2. Which item is exactly opposite the projector?
Ⓐ teacher's desk
Ⓑ books
● guided math table
Ⓓ my desk

3. How far from Lacee's desk is Rudi's desk?
4 feet

Write how you know.
Possible Answer: If you subtract the x-coordinates, you calculate 6 – 2 = 4.

76

Use a Coordinate Plane
The Number System

DIRECTIONS: Follow the steps below to make a map of Rudi's town. Each number on the axes represents 1 mile.

Strategy Create or refer to visuals as often as needed to understand and solve a problem.

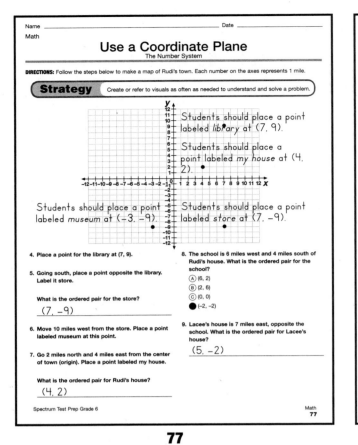

Students should place a point labeled *library* at (7, 9).

Students should place a point labeled *my house* at (4, 2).

Students should place a point labeled *museum* at (−3, −9).

Students should place a point labeled *store* at (7, −9).

4. Place a point for the library at (7, 9).

5. Going south, place a point opposite the library. Label it store.

What is the ordered pair for the store?

(7, −9)

6. Move 10 miles west from the store. Place a point labeled museum at this point.

7. Go 2 miles north and 4 miles east from the center of town (origin). Place a point labeled my house.

What is the ordered pair for Rudi's house?

(4, 2)

8. The school is 6 miles west and 4 miles south of Rudi's house. What is the ordered pair for the school?
Ⓐ (6, 2)
Ⓑ (2, 6)
Ⓒ (0, 0)
● (−2, −2)

9. Lacee's house is 7 miles east, opposite the school. What is the ordered pair for Lacee's house?

(5, −2)

Spectrum Test Prep Grade 6

Math 77

Evaluate Exponents
Expressions and Equations

DIRECTIONS: Choose or write the correct answer.

Strategy Evaluate expressions with exponents using multiplication.

Test Tip Remember that an exponent tells how many times to multiply the base by itself. For example, 7^3 means $7 \times 7 \times 7$, not 7×3.

1. Complete the table.

$2 \times 2 \times 2 \times 2 \times 2$	2^5
$3 \times 3 \times 3 \times 3$	3^4
8×8	8^2
$6 \times 6 \times 6$	6^3
$1 \times 1 \times 1 \times 1 \times 1 \times 1 \times 1$	1^7

2. What is the value of 8^4?
Ⓐ 32
Ⓑ 12
● 4,096
Ⓓ 16

Write how you used multiplication to find the answer.

Possible Answer: First, I multiplied 8×8 and found 64. Then, I multiplied 64×8 and found 512. Finally, I multiplied 512×64 and found 4,096.

3. A square has a side length of 5 feet. What exponent expression can you write to find the area?

5^2

What if the square were one side of cube? What exponent expression could you use to find the volume of the cube?

5^3

4. A clown is holding 6 balloons. Inside each balloon are 6 coins. On each coin are 6 dots. How many dots are there?
Ⓐ 18
Ⓑ 6
● 216
Ⓓ 36

Write how you found your answer.

Possible Answer: I knew that I would have to multiply $6 \times 6 \times 6$, which is 6^3. I multiplied 6×6 and found 36. Then, I multiplied that by another 6 and found 216.

5. Write a story like the one above for the expression 4^4.

Possible Answer: Once there were 4 trees. Each one had 4 leaves. Each leaf had 4 ladybugs. Each ladybug had 4 spots. How many spots were there?

Math 78

Spectrum Test Prep Grade 6

Understand Expressions
Expressions and Equations

DIRECTIONS: Choose or write the correct answer.

Strategy Write expressions to represent real-world situations, then evaluate the expressions to find unknown values.

1. Write an expression to represent y less than 5.

$5 - y$

2. Which expressions match the words *the sum of x and 7*? Choose two.
Ⓐ $x - 7$
Ⓑ $7x$
● $x + 7$
● $7 + x$

3. In the equation $3x + 7 = 22$, name the…
terms $3x, 7$
sum 22
coefficient 3
variable x

Test Tip Remember that a variable represents an unknown number.

4. Evaluate the expressions when $a = 5$, $b = 3$, and $c = 7$
$4a + b$ 23 $ac - 2b$ 29
$a(b + 4)$ 35 $a^2 - b^2$ 16

5. Use the formulas $V = s^3$ and $A = 6s^2$ to find the volume and surface area of a cube with sides of length $s = \frac{1}{2}$. Show your work.

$V = \boxed{\frac{1}{8}}$

$A = \boxed{1\frac{1}{2}}$

6. Evaluate $2a - 3b + 4c$, when $a = 4$, $b = 3$, and $c = 2$.
Ⓐ 25
Ⓑ 38
● 7
Ⓓ 12

7. Evaluate $3a + 4b + 6c$, when $a = 5$, $b = 4$, and $c = 3$.
● 13
Ⓑ 49
Ⓒ 19
Ⓓ 62

Spectrum Test Prep Grade 6

Math 79

Understanding Expressions
Expressions and Equations

Test Tip Find the variable in an expression or equation. Common variables to use are x, n, and y. Any letter can be used as a variable in an expression or equation.

8. Kate is twice as old as Nathaniel. Write an expression to show this relationship. Let Nathaniel's age = n.

Possible Answer: $2n$

9. Micah sold 3 times as many pizzas as Sadie and Jason sold altogether. Which expression shows this relationship?
Ⓐ $3 + s + j$
Ⓑ $(s + j) - 3$
● $3(s + j)$
Ⓓ $3sj$

10. Three children evenly shared $\frac{1}{2}$ bag of cookies. Which expressions show this relationship?
● $\frac{1}{2}c \div 3$
● $\frac{1}{2}c \times \frac{1}{3}$
● $3(\frac{1}{2}c)$
Ⓓ $\frac{\frac{1}{2}c}{3}$

11. Write a situation to match the expression $3k - 7$.

Possible Answer: Hayden saved up 3 weeks of allowance but then spent $7.

Evaluate the expression for $k = 3$.

2

12. In one town, police calculate speeding tickets with this formula: $50 + 10m$. The first 10 miles per hour over the speed limit is a flat $50 fine. For each additional mile per hour over the speed limit, there is an additional $10 charged. What would the speeding ticket be for a person traveling 60 miles per hour in a 35-mile-per-hour zone?

$200

What would the speeding ticket be for a person traveling 90 miles per hour in a 55-mile-per-hour zone?

$400

What would the speed ticket be for a person traveling 80 miles per hour in a 65-mile-per-hour zone?

$100

Math 80

Spectrum Test Prep Grade 6

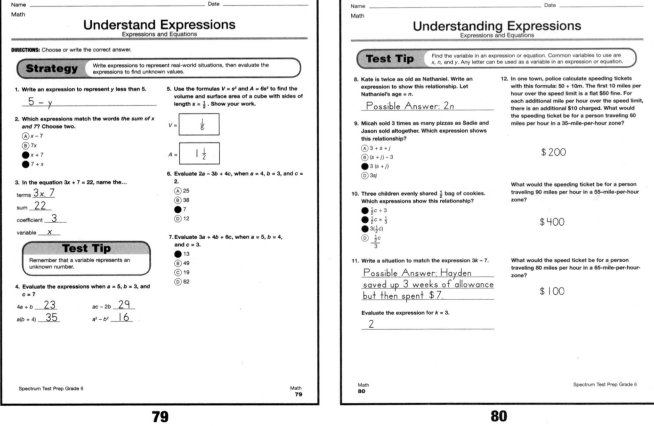

Answer Key

122

Spectrum Test Prep Grade 6

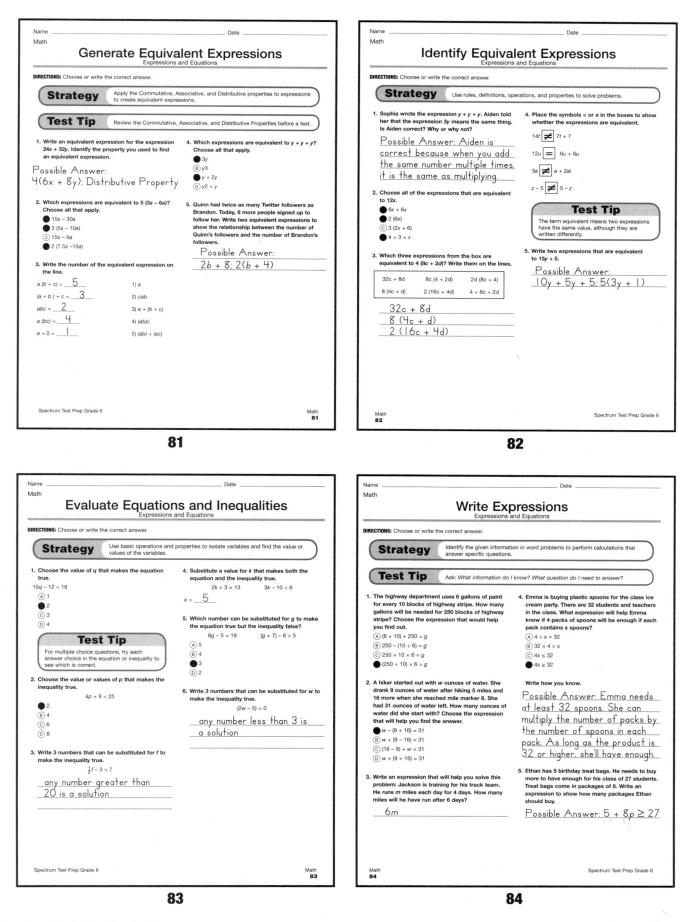

Page 81

Generate Equivalent Expressions
Expressions and Equations

DIRECTIONS: Choose or write the correct answer.

Strategy Apply the Commutative, Associative, and Distributive properties to expressions to create equivalent expressions.

Test Tip Review the Commutative, Associative, and Distributive Properties before a test.

1. Write an equivalent expression for the expression $24x + 32y$. Identify the property you used to find an equivalent expression.

Possible Answer:
$4(6x + 8y)$; Distributive Property

2. Which expressions are equivalent to $5(3s − 6a)$? Choose all that apply.
- ● $15s − 30a$
- $3(5s − 10a)$
- Ⓒ $15s − 6a$
- ● $2(7.5s − 15a)$

3. Write the number of the equivalent expression on the line.

$a(b + c) =$ __5__   1) a

$(a + b) + c =$ __3__   2) cab

$abc =$ __2__   3) $a + (b + c)$

$a(bc) =$ __4__   4) $(ab)c$

$a + 0 =$ __1__   5) $(ab) + (ac)$

4. Which expressions are equivalent to $y + y + y$? Choose all that apply.
- ● $3y$
- Ⓑ $y3$
- ● $y + 2y$
- Ⓓ $y2 + y$

5. Quinn had twice as many Twitter followers as Brandon. Today, 8 more people signed up to follow her. Write two equivalent expressions to show the relationship between the number of Quinn's followers and the number of Brandon's followers.

Possible Answer:
$2b + 8$; $2(b + 4)$

Page 82

Identify Equivalent Expressions
Expressions and Equations

DIRECTIONS: Choose or write the correct answer.

Strategy Use rules, definitions, operations, and properties to solve problems.

1. Sophia wrote the expression $y + y + y$. Aiden told her that the expression $3y$ means the same thing. Is Aiden correct? Why or why not?

Possible Answer: Aiden is
correct because when you add
the same number multiple times,
it is the same as multiplying.

2. Choose all of the expressions that are equivalent to $12x$.
- ● $6x + 6x$
- ● $2(6x)$
- Ⓒ $3(2x + 6)$
- ● $4 \times 3 \times x$

3. Which three expressions from the box are equivalent to $4(8c + 2d)$? Write them on the lines.

$32c + 8d$	$8c(4 + 2d)$	$2d(8c + 4)$
$8(4c + d)$	$2(16c + 4d)$	$4 \times 8c + 2d$

$32c + 8d$
$8(4c + d)$
$2(16c + 4d)$

4. Place the symbols = or ≠ in the boxes to show whether the expressions are equivalent.

$14t$ ≠ $7t + 7$

$12u$ = $6u + 6u$

$3a$ ≠ $a + 2ai$

$z − 5$ ≠ $5 − z$

Test Tip
The term equivalent means two expressions have the same value, although they are written differently.

5. Write two expressions that are equivalent to $15y + 5$.

Possible Answer:
$10y + 5y + 5$; $5(3y + 1)$

Page 83

Evaluate Equations and Inequalities
Expressions and Equations

DIRECTIONS: Choose or write the correct answer.

Strategy Use basic operations and properties to isolate variables and find the value or values of the variables.

1. Choose the value of q that makes the equation true.
$15q − 12 = 18$
- Ⓐ 1
- ● 2
- Ⓒ 3
- Ⓓ 4

Test Tip
For multiple choice questions, try each answer choice in the equation or inequality to see which is correct.

2. Choose the value or values of p that makes the inequality true.
$4p + 9 < 25$
- ● 2
- Ⓑ 4
- Ⓒ 6
- Ⓓ 8

3. Write 3 numbers that can be substituted for f to make the inequality true.
$\frac{1}{2}f − 3 > 7$

any number greater than
20 is a solution

4. Substitute a value for k that makes both the equation and the inequality true.
$2k + 3 = 13$ $3k − 10 < 6$
$k =$ __5__

5. Which number can be substituted for g to make the equation true but the inequality false?
$8g − 5 = 19$ $(g + 7) − 6 > 5$
- Ⓐ 5
- Ⓑ 4
- ● 3
- Ⓓ 2

6. Write 3 numbers that can be substituted for w to make the inequality true.
$(2w − 5) < 0$

any number less than 3 is
a solution

Page 84

Write Expressions
Expressions and Equations

DIRECTIONS: Choose or write the correct answer.

Strategy Identify the given information in word problems to perform calculations that answer specific questions.

Test Tip Ask: What information do I know? What question do I need to answer?

1. The highway department uses 6 gallons of paint for every 10 blocks of highway stripe. How many gallons will be needed for 250 blocks of highway stripe? Choose the expression that would help you find out.
- Ⓐ $(6 \times 10) + 250 = g$
- Ⓑ $250 − (10 \div 6) = g$
- Ⓒ $250 \times 10 \times 6 = g$
- ● $(250 \div 10) \times 6 = g$

2. A hiker started out with w ounces of water. She drank 9 ounces of water after hiking 5 miles and 16 more when she reached mile marker 8. She had 31 ounces of water left. How many ounces of water did she start with? Choose the expression that will help you find the answer.
- ● $w − (9 + 16) = 31$
- Ⓑ $w + (9 − 16) = 31$
- Ⓒ $(16 − 9) − w = 31$
- Ⓓ $w + (9 + 16) = 31$

3. Write an expression that will help you solve this problem: Jackson is training for his track team. He runs m miles each day for 4 days. How many miles will he have run after 6 days?

$6m$

4. Emma is buying plastic spoons for the class ice cream party. There are 32 students and teachers in the class. What expression will help Emma know if 4 packs of spoons will be enough if each pack contains s spoons?
- Ⓐ $4 \div s = 32$
- Ⓑ $32 \times 4 = s$
- Ⓒ $4s \leq 32$
- ● $4s \geq 32$

Write how you know.

Possible Answer: Emma needs
at least 32 spoons. She can
multiply the number of packs by
the number of spoons in each
pack. As long as the product is
32 or higher, she'll have enough.

5. Ethan has 5 birthday treat bags. He needs to buy more to have enough for his class of 27 students. Treat bags come in packages of 8. Write an expression to show how many packages Ethan should buy.

Possible Answer: $5 + 8p \geq 27$

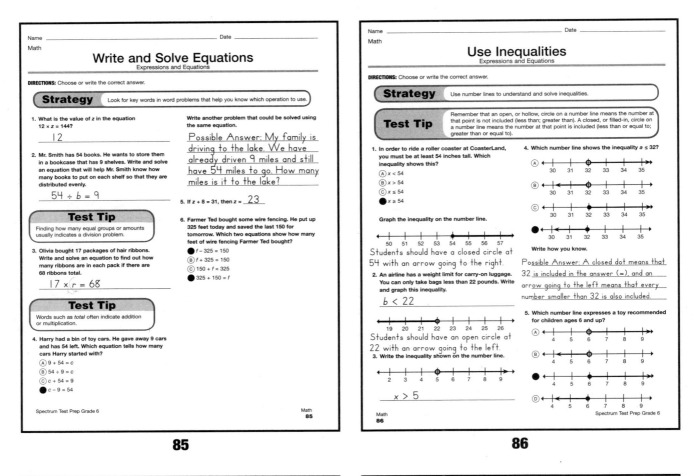

85

Write and Solve Equations
Expressions and Equations

DIRECTIONS: Choose or write the correct answer.

Strategy Look for key words in word problems that help you know which operation to use.

1. What is the value of *z* in the equation
$12 \times z = 144$?

___12___

2. Mr. Smith has 54 books. He wants to store them in a bookcase that has 9 shelves. Write and solve an equation that will help Mr. Smith know how many books to put on each shelf so that they are distributed evenly.

$54 \div b = 9$

Test Tip
Finding how many equal groups or amounts usually indicates a division problem.

3. Olivia bought 17 packages of hair ribbons. Write and solve an equation to find out how many ribbons are in each pack if there are 68 ribbons total.

$17 \times r = 68$

Test Tip
Words such as *total* often indicate addition or multiplication.

4. Harry had a bin of toy cars. He gave away 9 cars and has 54 left. Which equation tells how many cars Harry started with?
- (A) $9 + 54 = c$
- (B) $54 \div 9 = c$
- (C) $c + 54 = 9$
- ● $c - 9 = 54$

Write another problem that could be solved using the same equation.

Possible Answer: My family is driving to the lake. We have already driven 9 miles and still have 54 miles to go. How many miles is it to the lake?

5. If $z + 8 = 31$, then $z =$ ___23___

6. Farmer Ted bought some wire fencing. He put up 325 feet today and saved the last 150 for tomorrow. Which two equations show how many feet of wire fencing Farmer Ted bought?
- ● $f - 325 = 150$
- (B) $f + 325 = 150$
- (C) $150 + f = 325$
- ● $325 + 150 = f$

Spectrum Test Prep Grade 6

Math
85

86

Use Inequalities
Expressions and Equations

DIRECTIONS: Choose or write the correct answer.

Strategy Use number lines to understand and solve inequalities.

Test Tip
Remember that an open, or hollow, circle on a number line means the number at that point is not included (less than; greater than). A closed, or filled-in, circle on a number line means the number at that point is included (less than or equal to; greater than or equal to).

1. In order to ride a roller coaster at CoasterLand, you must be at least 54 inches tall. Which inequality shows this?
- (A) $x < 54$
- (B) $x > 54$
- (C) $x \le 54$
- ● $x \ge 54$

Graph the inequality on the number line.

Students should have a closed circle at 54 with an arrow going to the right.

2. An airline has a weight limit for carry-on luggage. You can only take bags less than 22 pounds. Write and graph this inequality.

$b < 22$

Students should have an open circle at 22 with an arrow going to the left.

3. Write the inequality shown on the number line.

$x > 5$

4. Which number line shows the inequality $a \le 32$?

Write how you know.

Possible Answer: A closed dot means that 32 is included in the answer (=), and an arrow going to the left means that every number smaller than 32 is also included.

5. Which number line expresses a toy recommended for children ages 6 and up?

Math
86

Spectrum Test Prep Grade 6

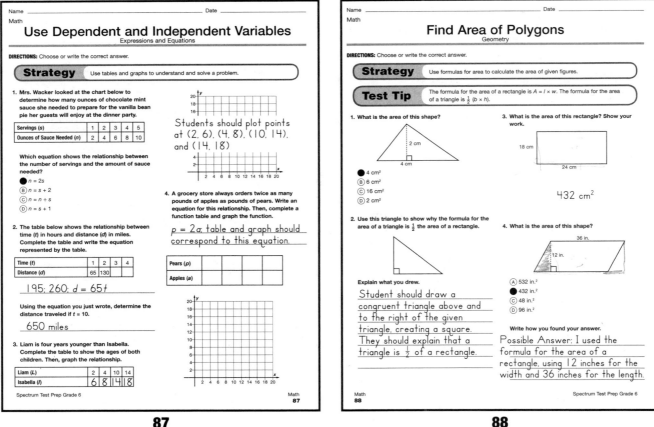

87

Use Dependent and Independent Variables
Expressions and Equations

DIRECTIONS: Choose or write the correct answer.

Strategy Use tables and graphs to understand and solve a problem.

1. Mrs. Wacker looked at the chart below to determine how many ounces of chocolate mint sauce she needed to prepare for the vanilla bean pie her guests will enjoy at the dinner party.

Servings (s)	1	2	3	4	5
Ounces of Sauce Needed (n)	2	4	6	8	10

Which equation shows the relationship between the number of servings and the amount of sauce needed?
- ● $n = 2s$
- (B) $n = s + 2$
- (C) $n = n \div s$
- (D) $n = s + 1$

2. The table below shows the relationship between time (*t*) in hours and distance (*d*) in miles. Complete the table and write the equation represented by the table.

Time (t)	1	2	3	4
Distance (d)	65	130		

$195; 260; d = 65t$

Using the equation you just wrote, determine the distance traveled if $t = 10$.

650 miles

3. Liam is four years younger than Isabella. Complete the table to show the ages of both children. Then, graph the relationship.

Liam (L)	2	4	10	14
Isabella (I)	6	8	14	18

Students should plot points at (2, 6), (4, 8), (10, 14), and (14, 18)

4. A grocery store always orders twice as many pounds of apples as pounds of pears. Write an equation for this relationship. Then, complete a function table and graph the function.

$p = 2a$; table and graph should correspond to this equation.

Pears (p)			
Apples (a)			

Spectrum Test Prep Grade 6

Math
87

88

Find Area of Polygons
Geometry

DIRECTIONS: Choose or write the correct answer.

Strategy Use formulas for area to calculate the area of given figures.

Test Tip
The formula for the area of a rectangle is $A = l \times w$. The formula for the area of a triangle is $\frac{1}{2}(b \times h)$.

1. What is the area of this shape?
- ● $4\ cm^2$
- (B) $6\ cm^2$
- (C) $16\ cm^2$
- (D) $2\ cm^2$

2. Use this triangle to show why the formula for the area of a triangle is $\frac{1}{2}$ the area of a rectangle.

Explain what you drew.

Student should draw a congruent triangle above and to the right of the given triangle, creating a square. They should explain that a triangle is $\frac{1}{2}$ of a rectangle.

3. What is the area of this rectangle? Show your work.

$432\ cm^2$

4. What is the area of this shape?
- (A) $532\ in.^2$
- ● $432\ in.^2$
- (C) $48\ in.^2$
- (D) $96\ in.^2$

Write how you found your answer.

Possible Answer: I used the formula for the area of a rectangle, using 12 inches for the width and 36 inches for the length.

Math
88

Spectrum Test Prep Grade 6

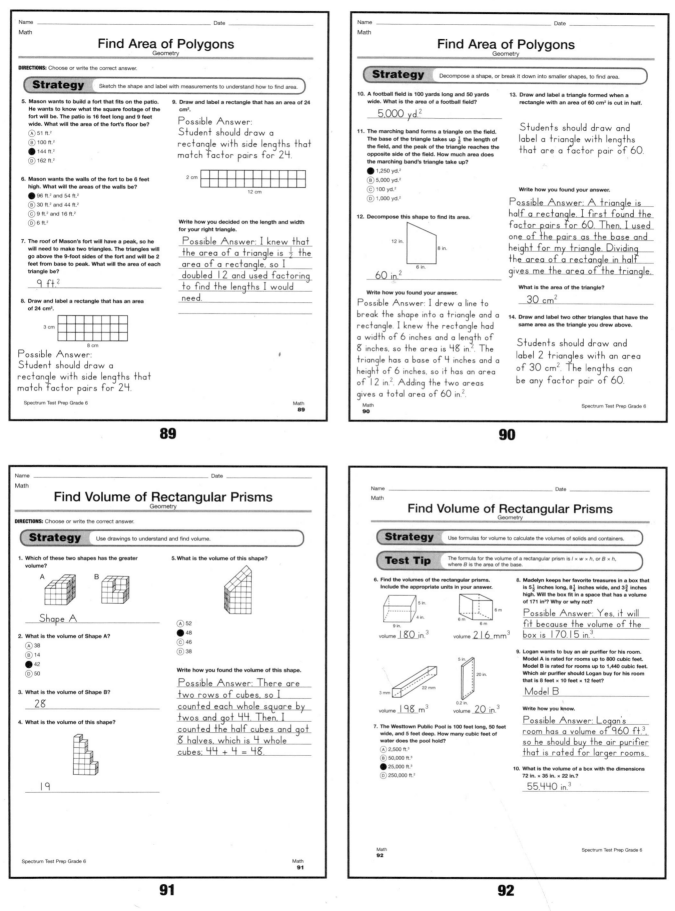

Page 89

Name _____ Date _____
Math

Find Area of Polygons
Geometry

DIRECTIONS: Choose or write the correct answer.

Strategy — Sketch the shape and label with measurements to understand how to find area.

5. Mason wants to build a fort that fits on the patio. He wants to know what the square footage of the fort will be. The patio is 16 feet long and 9 feet wide. What will be the area of the fort's floor be?
   - Ⓐ 51 ft.²
   - Ⓑ 100 ft.²
   - ● 144 ft.²
   - Ⓓ 162 ft.²

6. Mason wants the walls of the fort to be 6 feet high. What will the areas of the walls be?
   - ● 96 ft.² and 54 ft.²
   - Ⓑ 30 ft.² and 44 ft.²
   - Ⓒ 9 ft.² and 16 ft.²
   - Ⓓ 6 ft.²

7. The roof of Mason's fort will have a peak, so he will need to make two triangles. The triangles will go above the 9-foot sides of the fort and will be 2 feet from base to peak. What will the area of each triangle be?

   _9 ft.²_

8. Draw and label a rectangle that has an area of 24 cm².

   3 cm [grid] 8 cm

   Possible Answer:
   Student should draw a rectangle with side lengths that match factor pairs for 24.

9. Draw and label a rectangle that has an area of 24 cm².

   Possible Answer:
   Student should draw a rectangle with side lengths that match factor pairs for 24.

   2 cm [grid] 12 cm

   Write how you decided on the length and width for your right triangle.

   Possible Answer: I knew that the area of a triangle is ½ the area of a rectangle, so I doubled 12 and used factoring to find the lengths I would need.

Spectrum Test Prep Grade 6

Math
89

89

Page 90

Name _____ Date _____
Math

Find Area of Polygons
Geometry

Strategy — Decompose a shape, or break it down into smaller shapes, to find area.

10. A football field is 100 yards long and 50 yards wide. What is the area of a football field?

    _5,000 yd.²_

11. The marching band forms a triangle on the field. The base of the triangle takes up ½ the length of the field, and the peak of the triangle reaches the opposite side of the field. How much area does the marching band's triangle take up?
    - ● 1,250 yd.²
    - Ⓑ 5,000 yd.²
    - Ⓒ 100 yd.²
    - Ⓓ 1,000 yd.²

12. Decompose this shape to find its area.

    12 in. [shape] 8 in. 6 in.

    _60 in.²_

    Write how you found your answer.
    Possible Answer: I drew a line to break the shape into a triangle and a rectangle. I knew the rectangle had a width of 6 inches and a length of 8 inches, so the area is 48 in.². The triangle has a base of 4 inches and a height of 6 inches, so it has an area of 12 in.². Adding the two areas gives a total area of 60 in.².

13. Draw and label a triangle formed when a rectangle with an area of 60 cm² is cut in half.

    Students should draw and label a triangle with lengths that are a factor pair of 60.

    Write how you found your answer.
    Possible Answer: A triangle is half a rectangle. I first found the factor pairs for 60. Then, I used one of the pairs as the base and height for my triangle. Dividing the area of a rectangle in half gives me the area of the triangle.

    What is the area of the triangle?
    30 cm²

14. Draw and label two other triangles that have the same area as the triangle you drew above.

    Students should draw and label 2 triangles with an area of 30 cm². The lengths can be any factor pair of 60.

Math
90

Spectrum Test Prep Grade 6

90

Page 91

Name _____ Date _____
Math

Find Volume of Rectangular Prisms
Geometry

DIRECTIONS: Choose or write the correct answer.

Strategy — Use drawings to understand and find volume.

1. Which of these two shapes has the greater volume?

   A [cube figure] B [cube figure]

   Shape A

2. What is the volume of Shape A?
   - Ⓐ 38
   - Ⓑ 14
   - ● 42
   - Ⓓ 50

3. What is the volume of Shape B?

   _28_

4. What is the volume of this shape?

   [figure]

   _19_

5. What is the volume of this shape?

   [figure]

   - Ⓐ 52
   - ● 48
   - Ⓒ 46
   - Ⓓ 38

   Write how you found the volume of this shape.
   Possible Answer: There are two rows of cubes, so I counted each whole square by twos and got 44. Then, I counted the half cubes and got 8 halves, which is 4 whole cubes; 44 + 4 = 48.

Spectrum Test Prep Grade 6

Math
91

91

Page 92

Name _____ Date _____
Math

Find Volume of Rectangular Prisms
Geometry

Strategy — Use formulas for volume to calculate the volumes of solids and containers.

Test Tip — The formula for the volume of a rectangular prism is $l \times w \times h$, or $B \times h$, where B is the area of the base.

6. Find the volumes of the rectangular prisms. Include the appropriate units in your answer.

   [prism] 5 in. 9 in. 4 in.
   volume _180_ in.³

   [prism] 6 m 6 m 6 m
   volume _216_ mm³

   [prism] 3 mm 22 mm
   volume _198_ m³

   [prism] 5 in. 20 in. 0.2 in.
   volume _20_ in.³

7. The Westtown Public Pool is 100 feet long, 50 feet wide, and 5 feet deep. How many cubic feet of water does the pool hold?
   - Ⓐ 2,500 ft.³
   - Ⓑ 50,000 ft.³
   - ● 25,000 ft.³
   - Ⓓ 250,000 ft.³

8. Madelyn keeps her favorite treasures in a box that is 5½ inches long, 8¼ inches wide, and 3⅜ inches high. Will the box fit in a space that has a volume of 171 in³? Why or why not?

   Possible Answer: Yes, it will fit because the volume of the box is 170.15 in.³.

9. Logan wants to buy an air purifier for his room. Model A is rated for rooms up to 800 cubic feet. Model B is rated for rooms up to 1,440 cubic feet. Which air purifier should Logan buy for his room that is 8 feet × 10 feet × 12 feet?

   Model B

   Write how you know.
   Possible Answer: Logan's room has a volume of 960 ft.³, so he should buy the air purifier that is rated for larger rooms.

10. What is the volume of a box with the dimensions 72 in. × 35 in. × 22 in.?

    _55,440_ in.³

Math
92

Spectrum Test Prep Grade 6

92

Draw Polygons in the Coordinate Plane
Geometry

DIRECTIONS: Choose or write the correct answer.

Strategy Graph data to visualize how numbers can describe two- and three-dimensional figures.

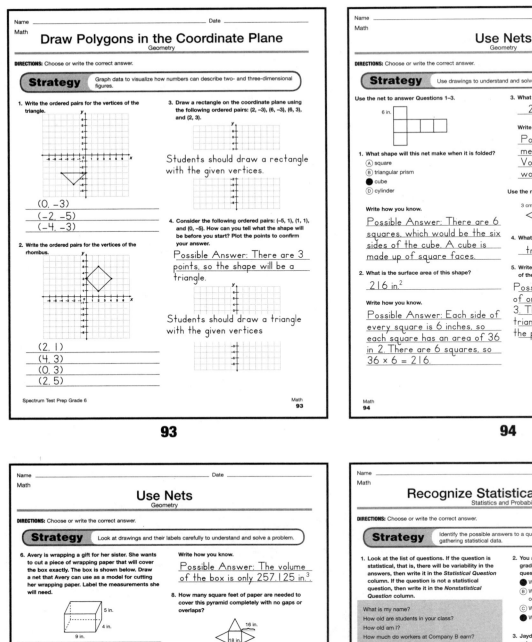

1. Write the ordered pairs for the vertices of the triangle.

(0, –3)
(–2, –5)
(–4, –3)

2. Write the ordered pairs for the vertices of the rhombus.

(2, 1)
(4, 3)
(0, 3)
(2, 5)

3. Draw a rectangle on the coordinate plane using the following ordered pairs: (2, –3), (6, –3), (6, 3), and (2, 3).

Students should draw a rectangle with the given vertices.

4. Consider the following ordered pairs: (–5, 1), (1, 1), and (0, –5). How can you tell what the shape will be before you start? Plot the points to confirm your answer.

Possible Answer: There are 3 points, so the shape will be a triangle.

Students should draw a triangle with the given vertices

93

Use Nets
Geometry

DIRECTIONS: Choose or write the correct answer.

Strategy Use drawings to understand and solve a problem.

Use the net to answer Questions 1–3.

6 in.

1. What shape will this net make when it is folded?
   Ⓐ square
   Ⓑ triangular prism
   ● cube
   Ⓓ cylinder

   Write how you know.

   Possible Answer: There are 6 squares, which would be the six sides of the cube. A cube is made up of square faces.

2. What is the surface area of this shape?

   216 in.²

   Write how you know.

   Possible Answer: Each side of every square is 6 inches, so each square has an area of 36 in 2. There are 6 squares, so 36 × 6 = 216.

3. What is the volume of this shape?

   216 in.³

   Write how you know.

   Possible Answer: All of the measurements are 6 inches. Volume is l × w × h, which would be 6 × 6 × 6 = 216.

Use the net to answer questions 4–5.

3 cm   2.6 cm

4. What shape will this net make when it is folded?

   triangular prism

5. Write how you can find the surface area of the shape.

   Possible Answer: Find the area of one rectangle and multiply by 3. Then, find the area of one triangle and multiply by 2. Add the products.

94

Use Nets
Geometry

DIRECTIONS: Choose or write the correct answer.

Strategy Look at drawings and their labels carefully to understand and solve a problem.

6. Avery is wrapping a gift for her sister. She wants to cut a piece of wrapping paper that will cover the box exactly. The box is shown below. Draw a net that Avery can use as a model for cutting her wrapping paper. Label the measurements she will need.

5 in.
4 in.
9 in.

Students should show a net with four interior rectangles measuring 9 in. × 4 in. There should be 2 end rectangles along the 4 in. side with a height of 5 in.

7. Cole went to the store to buy a box to ship a set of books to his friend. He found this box, which he has to put together.

5½ in.
8½ in.

The book set comes in a box with a volume of 258 in.³. Will this box be large enough to ship the books?

No

Write how you know.

Possible Answer: The volume of the box is only 257.125 in.³.

8. How many square feet of paper are needed to cover this pyramid completely with no gaps or overlaps?

16 in.
18 in.

900 in.²

95

Recognize Statistical Questions
Statistics and Probability

DIRECTIONS: Choose or write the correct answer.

Strategy Identify the possible answers to a question to determine if it would be useful for gathering statistical data.

1. Look at the list of questions. If the question is statistical, that is, there will be variability in the answers, then write it in the *Statistical Question* column. If the question is not a statistical question, then write it in the *Nonstatistical Question* column.

What is my name?
How old are students in your class?
How old am I?
How much do workers at Company B earn?
What color shirts are sixth graders wearing?
What color shirt am I wearing?
When is my birthday?
In which month do the most birthdays occur?

Statistical Question	Nonstatistical Question
How old are students in your class?	What is my name?
How much do workers at Company B earn?	How old am I?
What color shirts are sixth graders wearing?	What color shirt am I wearing?
In which month do the most birthdays occur?	When is my birthday?

2. You are doing a survey to find out about sixth graders' favorite foods. Which are good statistical questions? Choose all that apply.
   ● What kinds of food do you most like to eat?
   Ⓑ Which of these is your favorite: pizza or hot dogs?
   Ⓒ What did you eat for dinner last night?
   ● What is your favorite food?

3. Jayden stood outside a Mexican restaurant and asked customers going in what their favorite food is. Is this a good way for him to collect statistical data on favorite foods? Explain your answer.

   Possible Answer: No, because he is limiting his questions to people who are already planning to eat a particular type of food.

4. What would be the best way to collect data about students' favorite television shows?
   Ⓐ Ask your three best friends what their favorite shows are.
   Ⓑ Look online to see what the top rated shows are.
   ● Ask students in your school to participate in a survey.
   Ⓓ Post a question on your social media page.

96

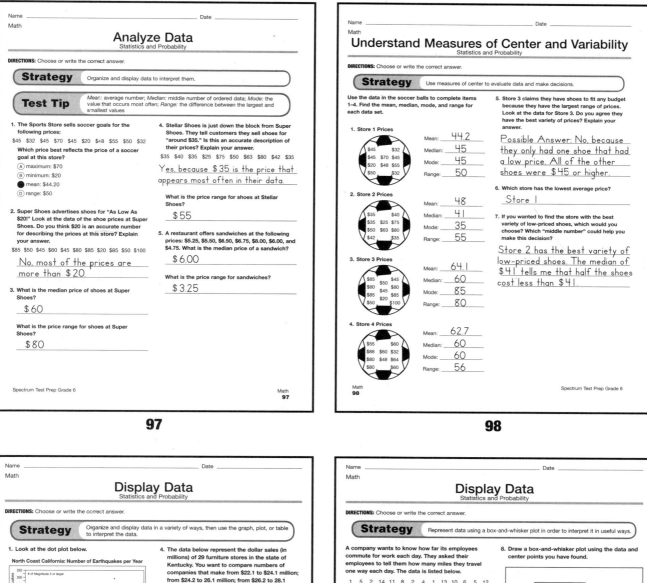

Page 97

Name _____ Date _____
Math

Analyze Data
Statistics and Probability

DIRECTIONS: Choose or write the correct answer.

Strategy — Organize and display data to interpret them.

Test Tip — *Mean:* average number; *Median:* middle number of ordered data; *Mode:* the value that occurs most often; *Range:* the difference between the largest and smallest values

1. The Sports Store sells soccer goals for the following prices:

$45 $32 $45 $70 $45 $20 $48 $55 $50 $32

Which price best reflects the price of a soccer goal at this store?
- (A) maximum: $70
- (B) minimum: $20
- ● mean: $44.20
- (D) range: $50

2. Super Shoes advertises shoes for "As Low As $20!" Look at the data of the shoe prices at Super Shoes. Do you think that $20 is an accurate number for describing the prices at this store? Explain your answer.

$85 $50 $45 $60 $45 $80 $85 $20 $85 $50 $100

No, most of the prices are more than $20.

3. What is the median price of shoes at Super Shoes?

$60

What is the price range for shoes at Super Shoes?

$80

4. Stellar Shoes is just down the block from Super Shoes. They tell customers they sell shoes for "around $35." Is this an accurate description of their prices? Explain your answer.

$35 $40 $35 $25 $75 $50 $63 $80 $42 $35

Yes, because $35 is the price that appears most often in their data.

What is the price range for shoes at Stellar Shoes?

$55

5. A restaurant offers sandwiches at the following prices: $5.25, $5.50, $6.50, $6.75, $8.00, $6.00, and $4.75. What is the median price of a sandwich?

$6.00

What is the price range for sandwiches?

$3.25

Spectrum Test Prep Grade 6

Math
97

Page 98

Name _____ Date _____
Math

Understand Measures of Center and Variability
Statistics and Probability

DIRECTIONS: Choose or write the correct answer.

Strategy — Use measures of center to evaluate data and make decisions.

Use the data in the soccer balls to complete items 1–4. Find the mean, median, mode, and range for each data set.

1. Store 1 Prices
$45 $32 $45 $70 $45 $20 $48 $55 $50 $32
Mean: 44.2
Median: 45
Mode: 45
Range: 50

2. Store 2 Prices
$35 $40 $35 $25 $75 $50 $63 $80 $42 $35
Mean: 48
Median: 41
Mode: 35
Range: 55

3. Store 3 Prices
$85 $50 $45 $60 $45 $80 $85 $85 $50 $20 $100
Mean: 64.1
Median: 60
Mode: 85
Range: 80

4. Store 4 Prices
$55 $60 $88 $60 $32 $80 $48 $64 $80 $60
Mean: 62.7
Median: 60
Mode: 60
Range: 56

5. Store 3 claims they have shoes to fit any budget because they have the largest range of prices. Look at the data for Store 3. Do you agree they have the best variety of prices? Explain your answer.

Possible Answer: No, because they only had one shoe that had a low price. All of the other shoes were $45 or higher.

6. Which store has the lowest average price?

Store 1

7. If you wanted to find the store with the best variety of low-priced shoes, which would you choose? Which "middle number" could help you make this decision?

Store 2 has the best variety of low-priced shoes. The median of $41 tells me that half the shoes cost less than $41.

Math
98

Spectrum Test Prep Grade 6

Page 99

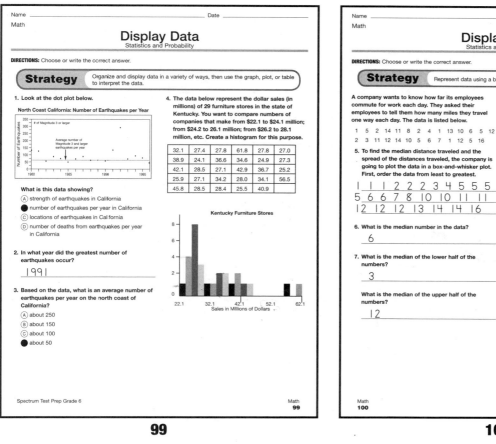

Name _____ Date _____
Math

Display Data
Statistics and Probability

DIRECTIONS: Choose or write the correct answer.

Strategy — Organize and display data in a variety of ways, then use the graph, plot, or table to interpret the data.

1. Look at the dot plot below.

North Coast California: Number of Earthquakes per Year

What is this data showing?
- (A) strength of earthquakes in California
- ● number of earthquakes per year in California
- (C) locations of earthquakes in California
- (D) number of deaths from earthquakes per year in California

2. In what year did the greatest number of earthquakes occur?

1991

3. Based on the data, what is an average number of earthquakes per year on the north coast of California?
- (A) about 250
- (B) about 150
- (C) about 100
- ● about 50

4. The data below represent the dollar sales (in millions) of 29 furniture stores in the state of Kentucky. You want to compare numbers of companies that make from $22.1 to $24.1 million; from $24.2 to 26.1 million; from $26.2 to 28.1 million, etc. Create a histogram for this purpose.

32.1	27.4	27.8	61.8	27.8	27.0
38.9	24.1	36.6	34.6	24.9	27.3
42.1	28.5	27.1	42.9	36.7	25.2
25.9	27.1	34.2	28.0	34.1	56.5
45.8	28.5	28.4	25.5	40.9

Kentucky Furniture Stores

Sales in Millions of Dollars

Spectrum Test Prep Grade 6

Math
99

Page 100

Name _____ Date _____
Math

Display Data
Statistics and Probability

DIRECTIONS: Choose or write the correct answer.

Strategy — Represent data using a box-and-whisker plot in order to interpret it in useful ways.

A company wants to know how far its employees commute for work each day. They asked their employees to tell them how many miles they travel one way each day. The data is listed below.

1 5 2 14 11 8 2 4 1 13 10 6 5 12
2 3 11 12 14 10 5 6 7 1 12 5 16

5. To find the median distance traveled and the spread of the distances traveled, the company is going to plot the data in a box-and-whisker plot. First, order the data from least to greatest.

1 1 1 2 2 2 3 4 5 5 5
5 6 6 7 8 10 10 11 11
12 12 12 13 14 14 16

6. What is the median number in the data?

6

7. What is the median of the lower half of the numbers?

3

What is the median of the upper half of the numbers?

12

8. Draw a box-and-whisker plot using the data and center points you have found.

0 2 4 6 8 10 12 14 16 18 20

Math
100

Spectrum Test Prep Grade 6

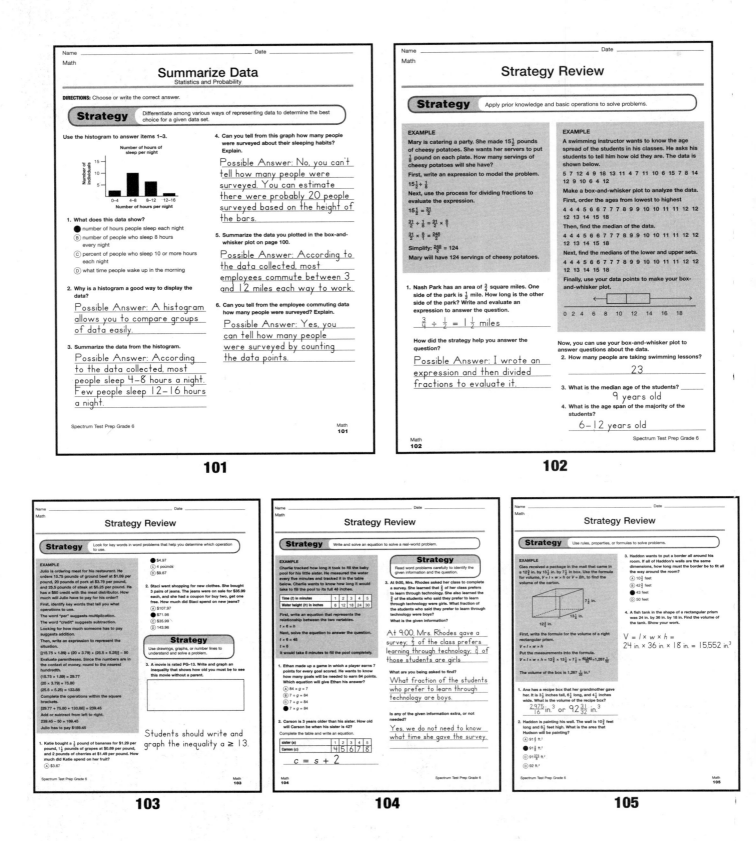

3190105927321 1